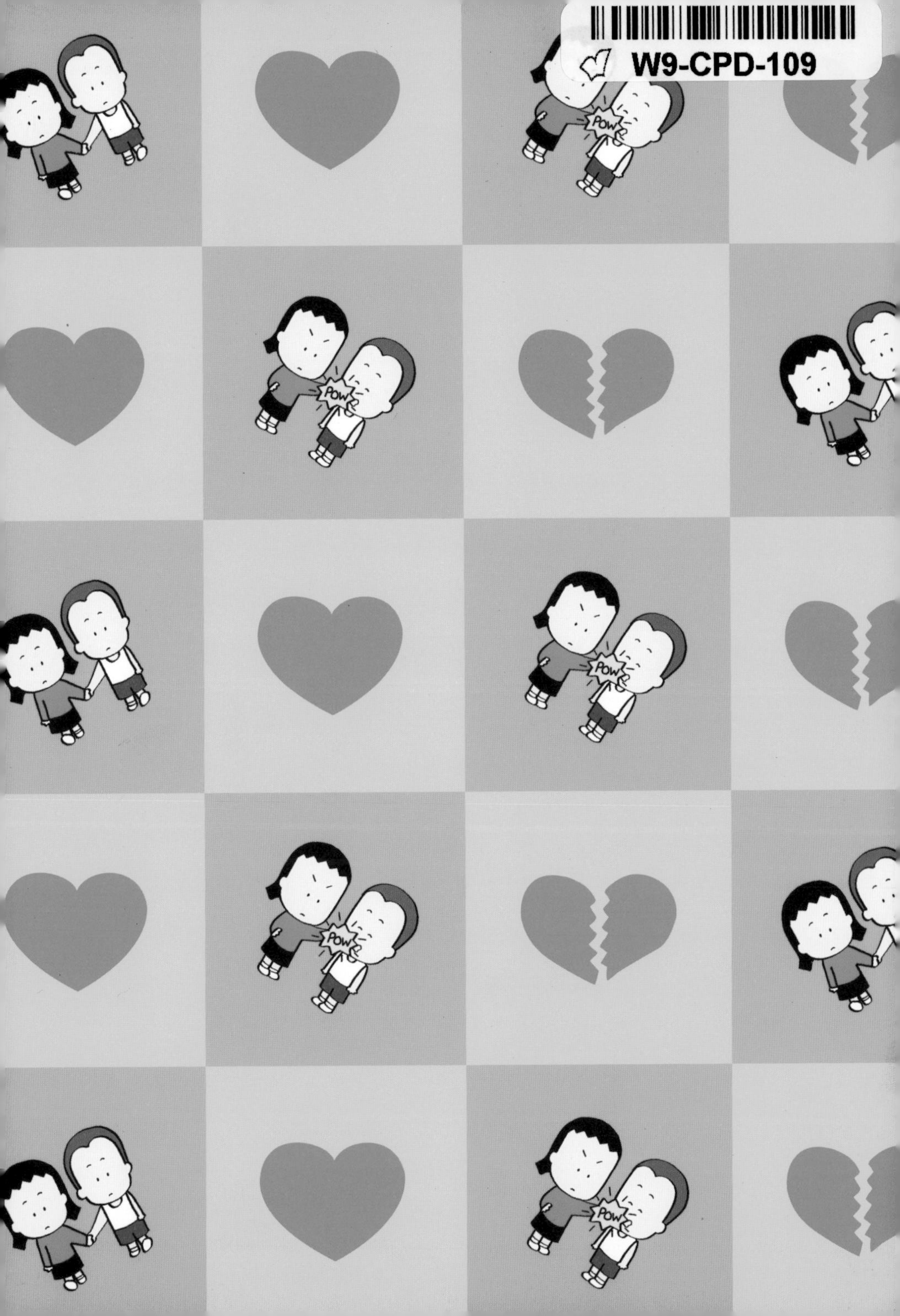
POW
POW
POW
POW
POW
POW

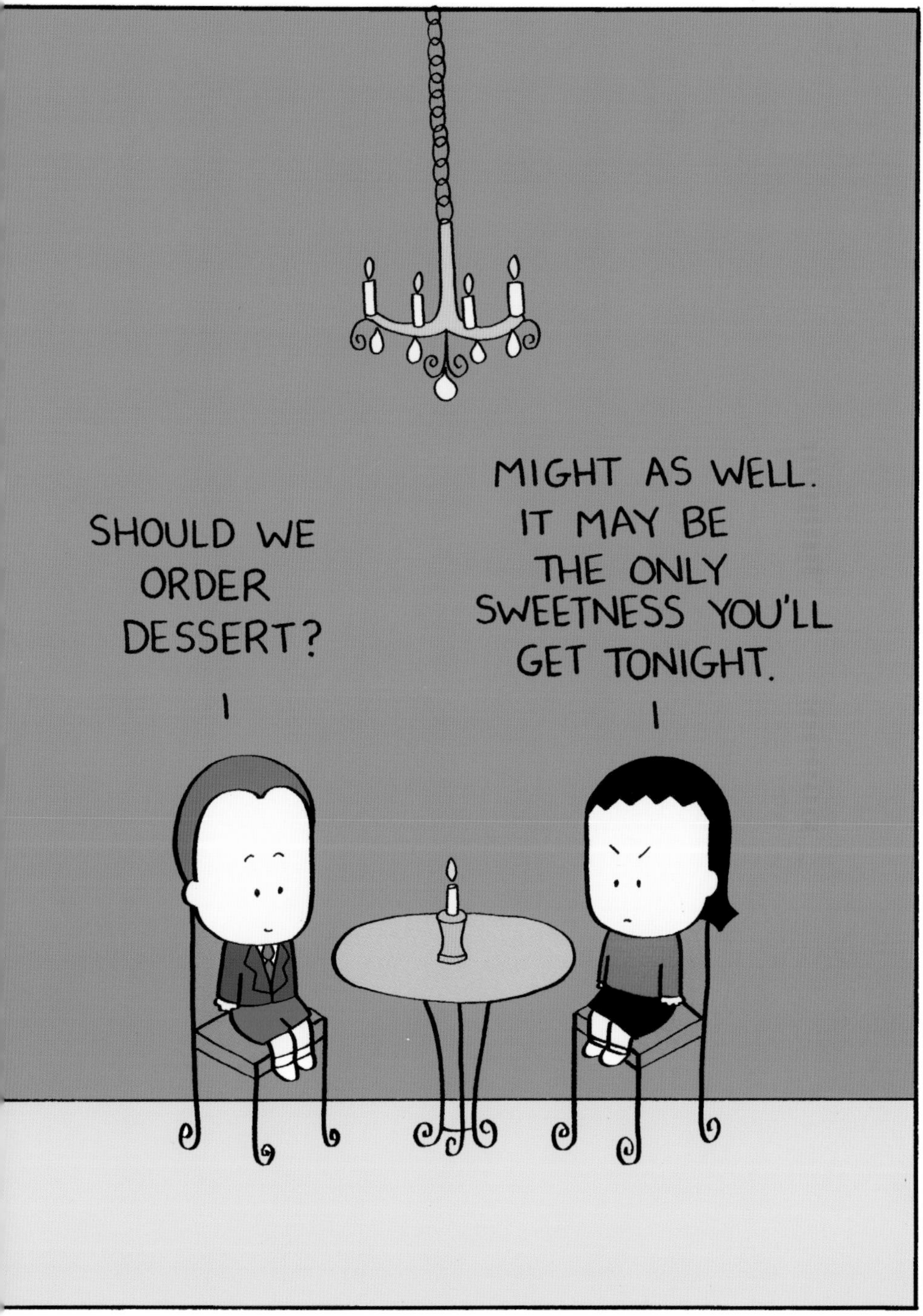
SHOULD WE ORDER DESSERT?
MIGHT AS WELL. IT MAY BE THE ONLY SWEETNESS YOU'LL GET TONIGHT.

ANGRY
LITTLE GIRLS

♥ IN LOVE ♥

by Lela Lee

ABRAMS, NEW YORK

Library of Congress Cataloging-in-Publication Data:
Lee, Lela.
Angry little girls in love / by Lela Lee.
p. cm.
ISBN 978-0-8109-7275-9
1. Comic books, strips, etc. I. Title.
PN6727.L385A57 2008
741.5'6973--dc22
2008002958

Text and illustrations copyright © 2008 Lela Lee
Editor: Tamar Brazis
Designer: Vivian Kimball

Printed and bound in China
10 9 8 7 6 5 4 3 2 1

HNA ▌▌▌▌▌
harry n. abrams, inc.
a subsidiary of La Martinière Groupe
115 West 18th Street
New York, NY 10011
www.hnabooks.com

FOR SPENCER

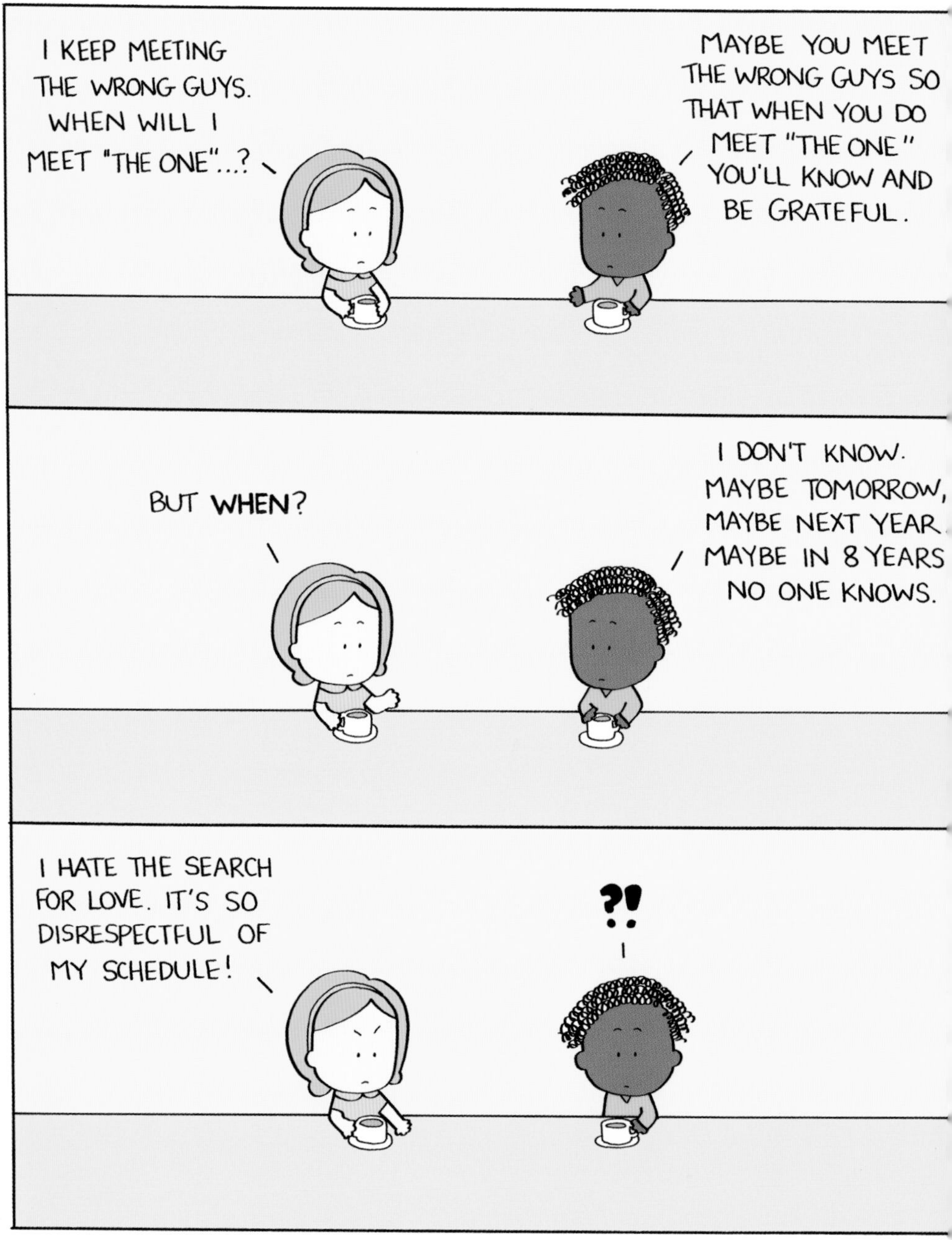
I KEEP MEETING THE WRONG GUYS. WHEN WILL I MEET "THE ONE"...?
MAYBE YOU MEET THE WRONG GUYS SO THAT WHEN YOU DO MEET "THE ONE" YOU'LL KNOW AND BE GRATEFUL.
BUT **WHEN**?
I DON'T KNOW. MAYBE TOMORROW, MAYBE NEXT YEAR. MAYBE IN 8 YEARS NO ONE KNOWS.
I HATE THE SEARCH FOR LOVE. IT'S SO DISRESPECTFUL OF MY SCHEDULE!
?!

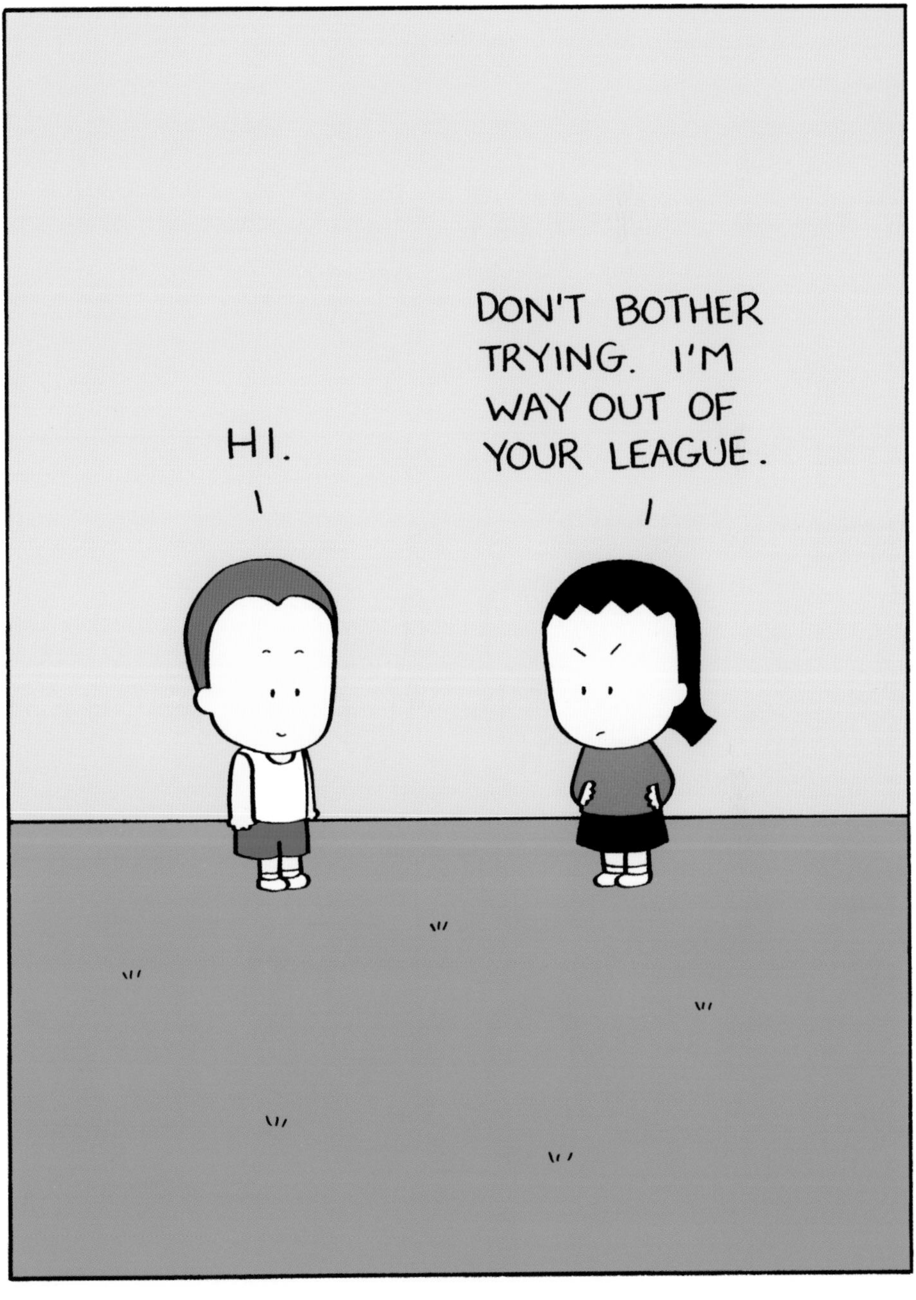
HI.
DON'T BOTHER TRYING. I'M WAY OUT OF YOUR LEAGUE.

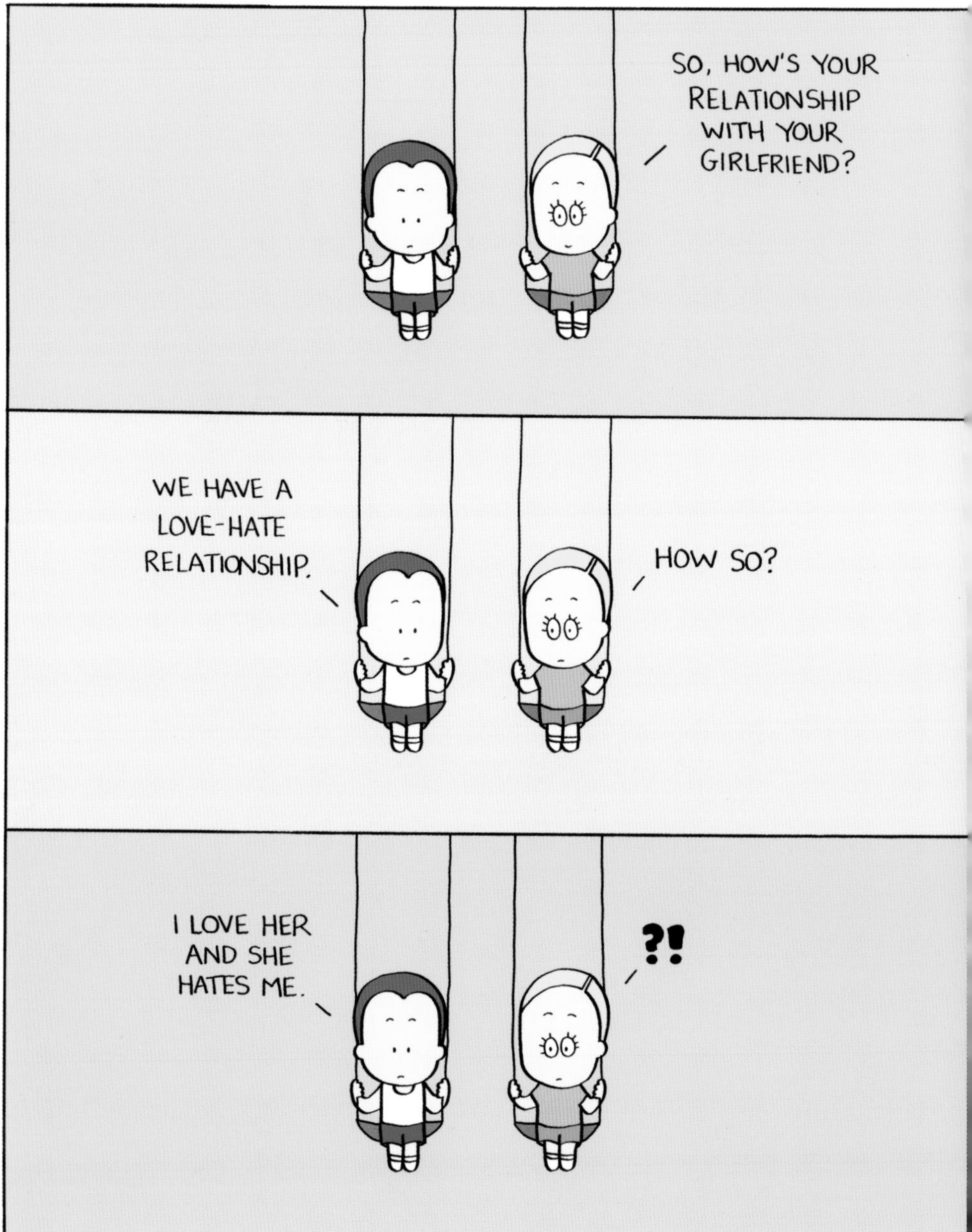

SO, HOW'S YOUR RELATIONSHIP WITH YOUR GIRLFRIEND?
WE HAVE A LOVE-HATE RELATIONSHIP.
HOW SO?
I LOVE HER AND SHE HATES ME.
?!

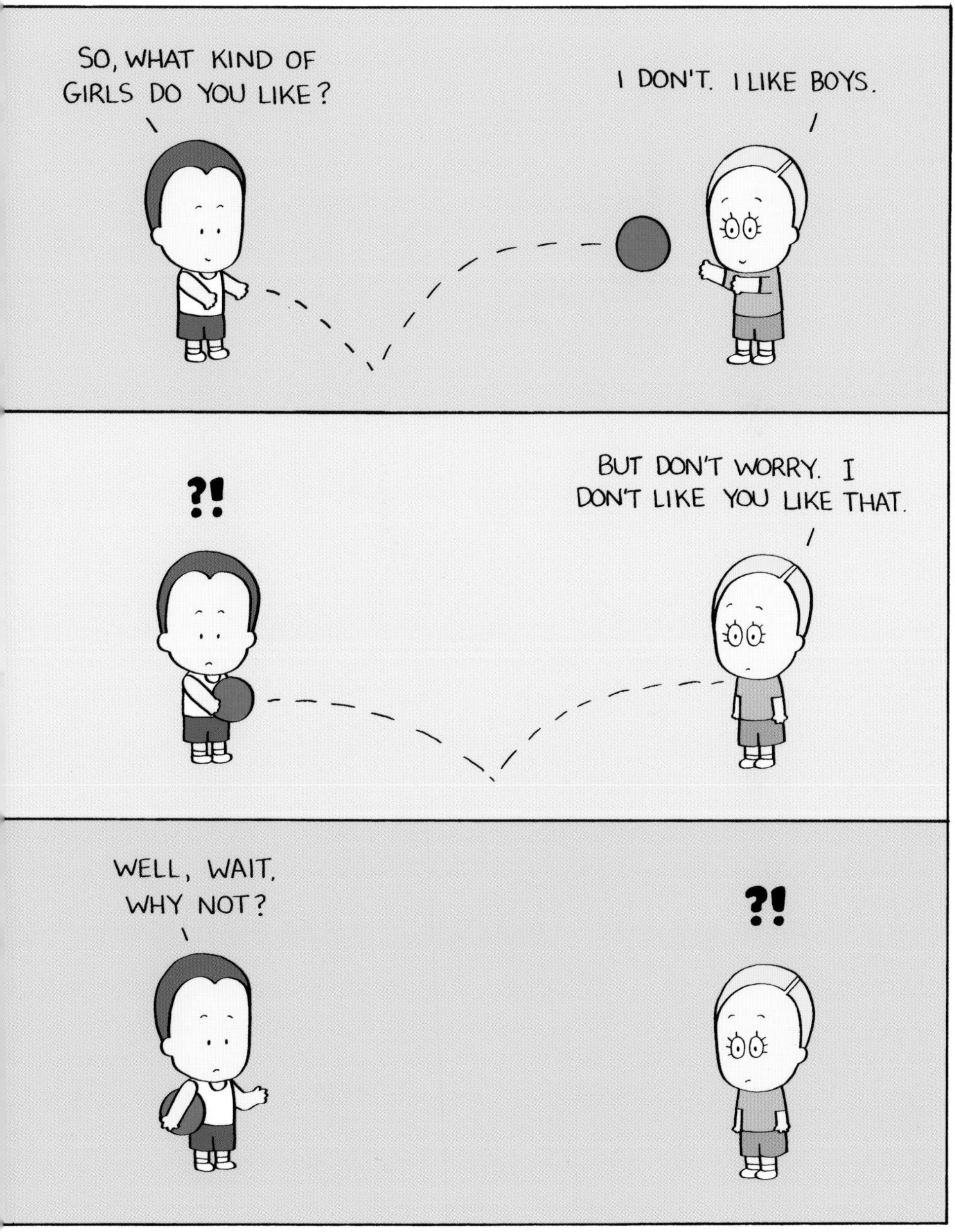
SO, WHAT KIND OF GIRLS DO YOU LIKE?
I DON'T. I LIKE BOYS.
?!
BUT DON'T WORRY. I DON'T LIKE YOU LIKE THAT.
WELL, WAIT, WHY NOT?
?!

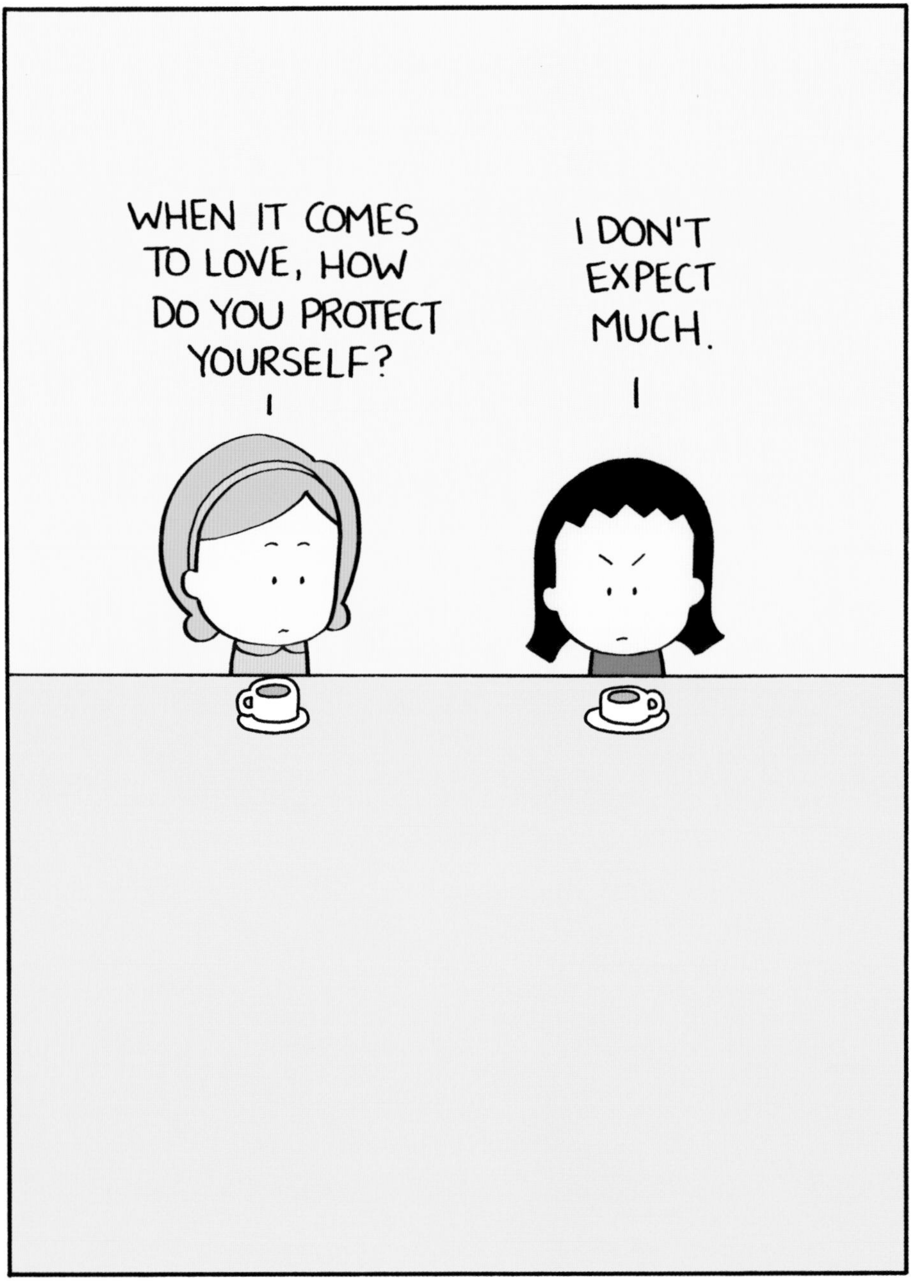
WHEN IT COMES TO LOVE, HOW DO YOU PROTECT YOURSELF?
I DON'T EXPECT MUCH.

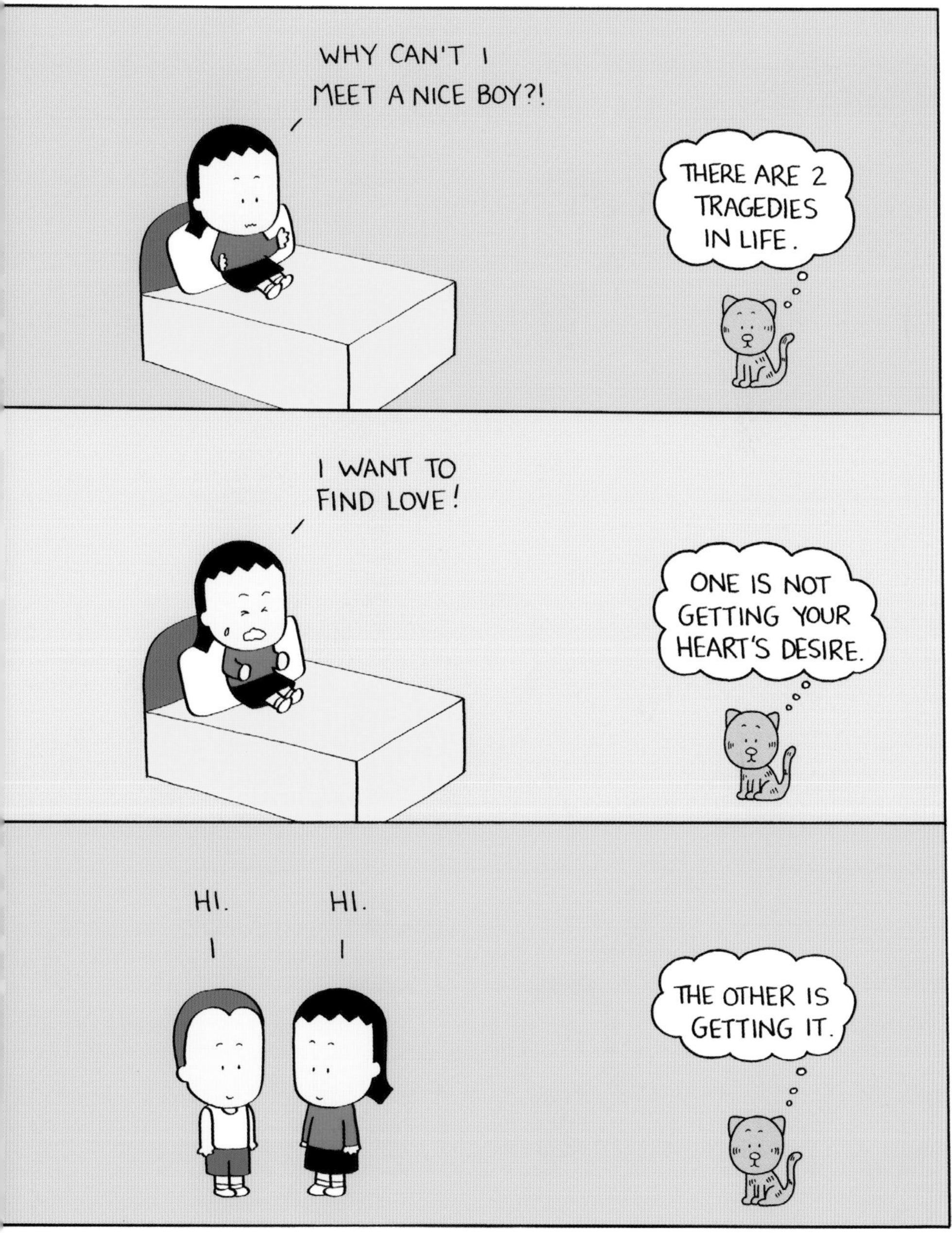
WHY CAN'T I MEET A NICE BOY?!
THERE ARE 2 TRAGEDIES IN LIFE.
I WANT TO FIND LOVE!
ONE IS NOT GETTING YOUR HEART'S DESIRE.
HI.
HI.
THE OTHER IS GETTING IT.

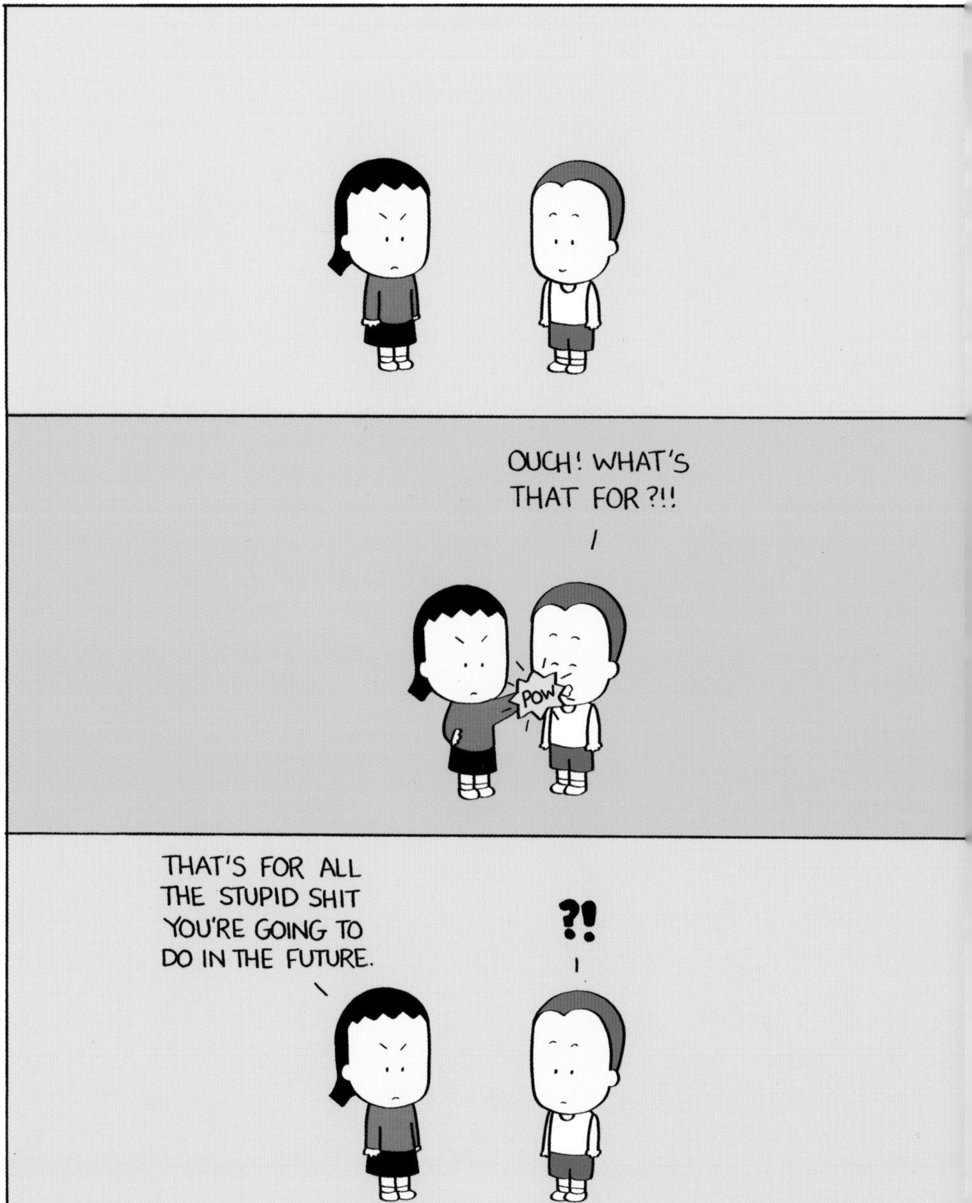
OUCH! WHAT'S THAT FOR?!!
POW
THAT'S FOR ALL THE STUPID SHIT YOU'RE GOING TO DO IN THE FUTURE.
?!

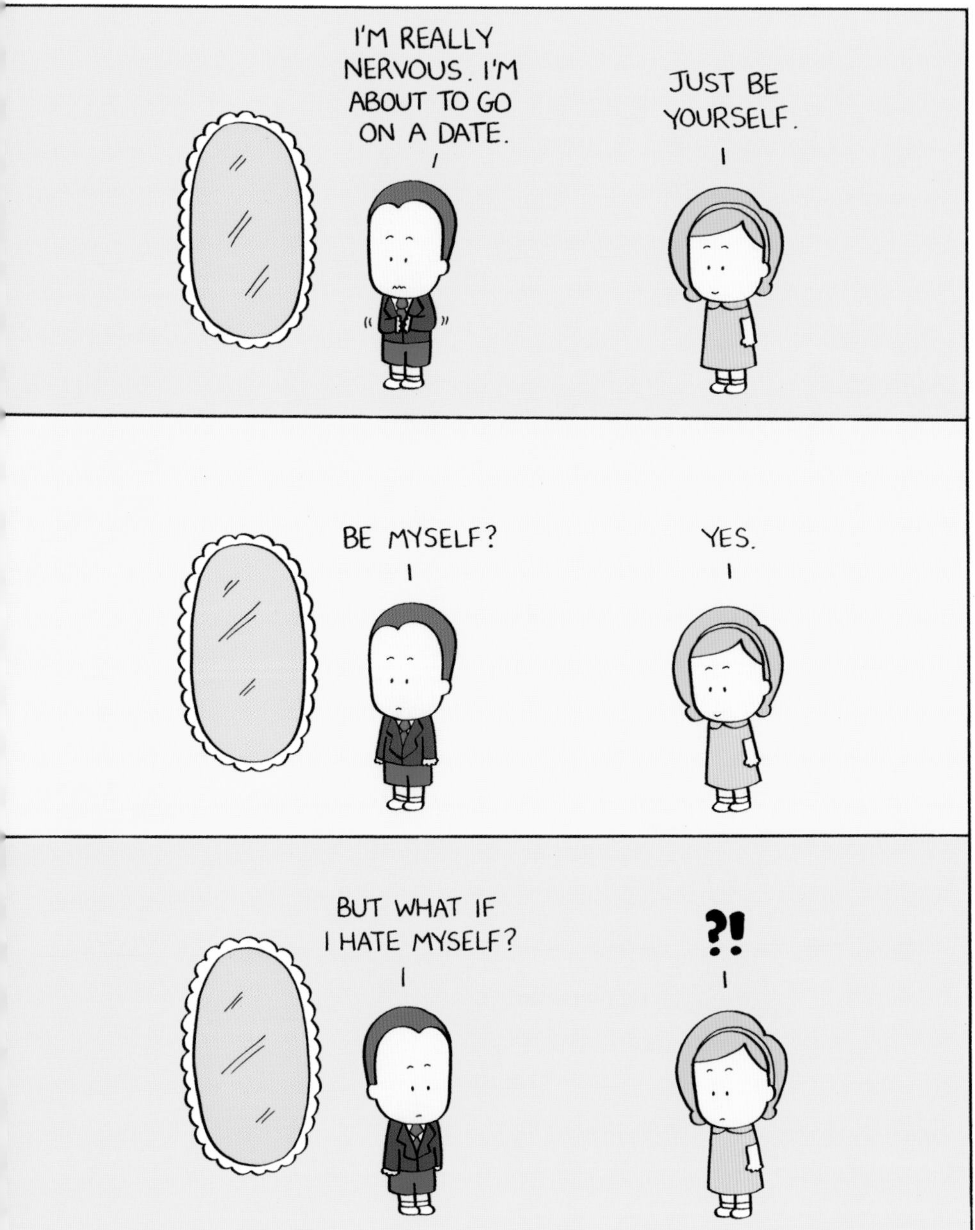
I'M REALLY NERVOUS. I'M ABOUT TO GO ON A DATE.
JUST BE YOURSELF.
BE MYSELF?
YES.
BUT WHAT IF I HATE MYSELF?
?!

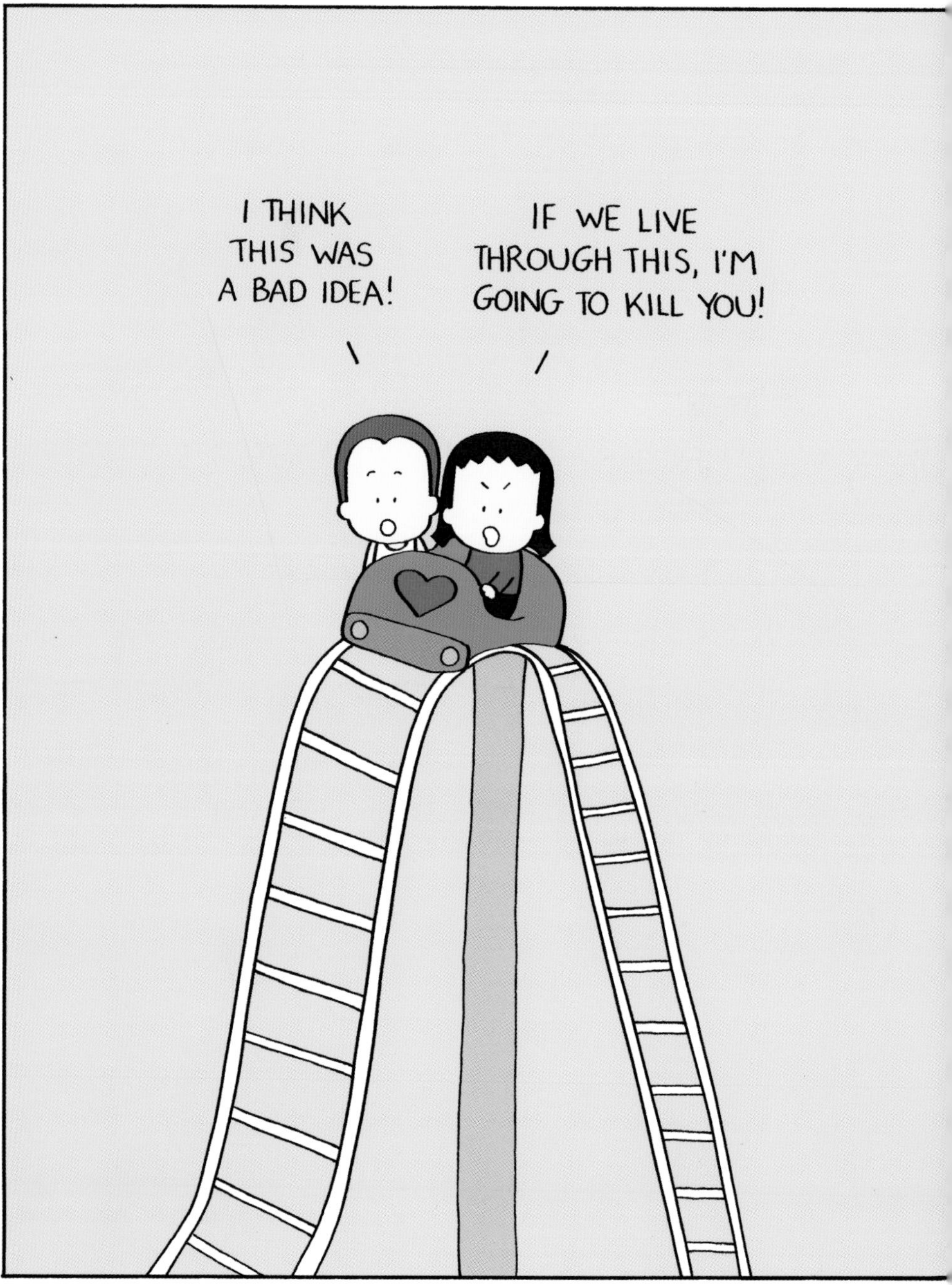
I THINK THIS WAS A BAD IDEA!
IF WE LIVE THROUGH THIS, I'M GOING TO KILL YOU!

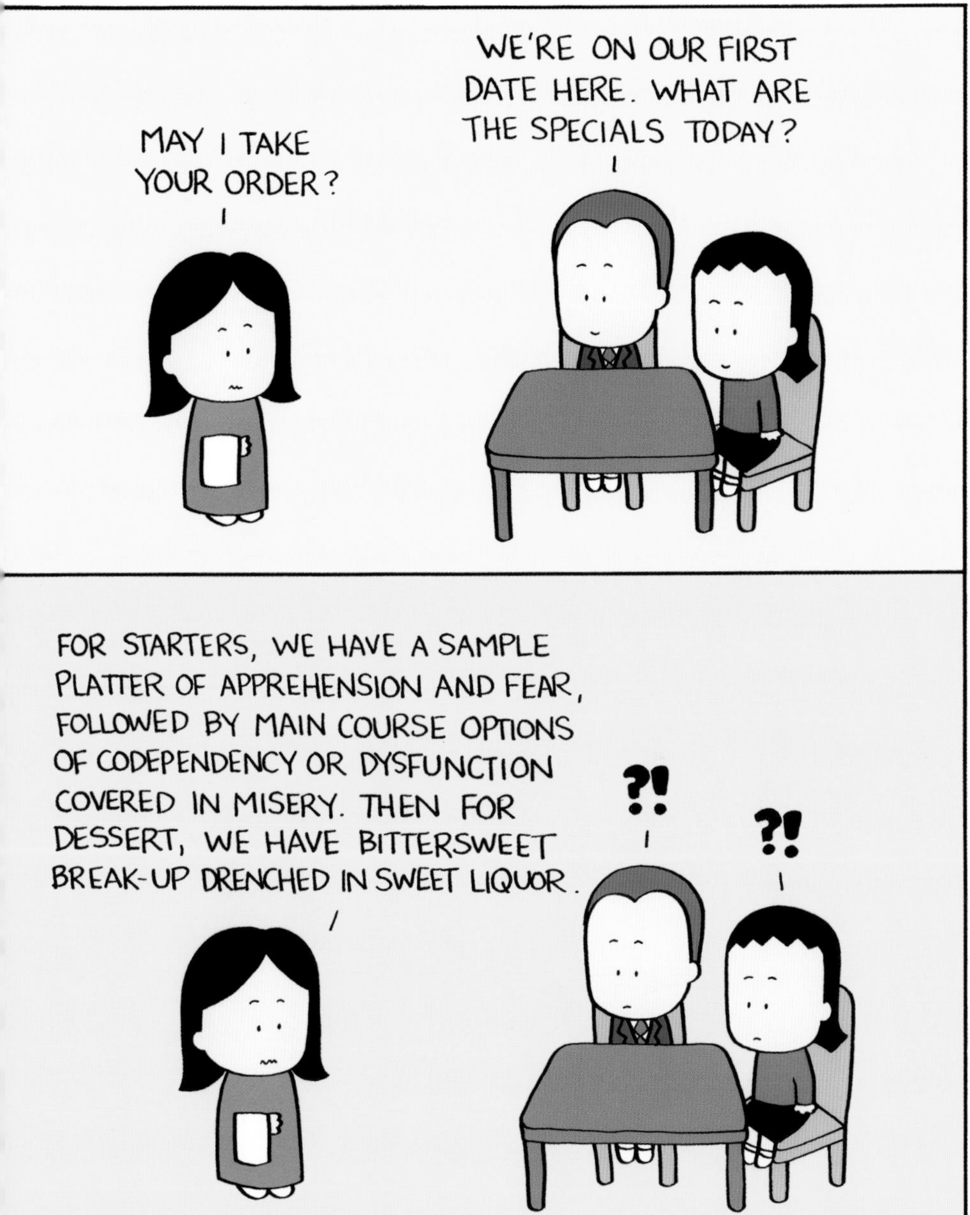
MAY I TAKE YOUR ORDER?
WE'RE ON OUR FIRST DATE HERE. WHAT ARE THE SPECIALS TODAY?
FOR STARTERS, WE HAVE A SAMPLE PLATTER OF APPREHENSION AND FEAR, FOLLOWED BY MAIN COURSE OPTIONS OF CODEPENDENCY OR DYSFUNCTION COVERED IN MISERY. THEN FOR DESSERT, WE HAVE BITTERSWEET BREAK-UP DRENCHED IN SWEET LIQUOR.
?!
?!

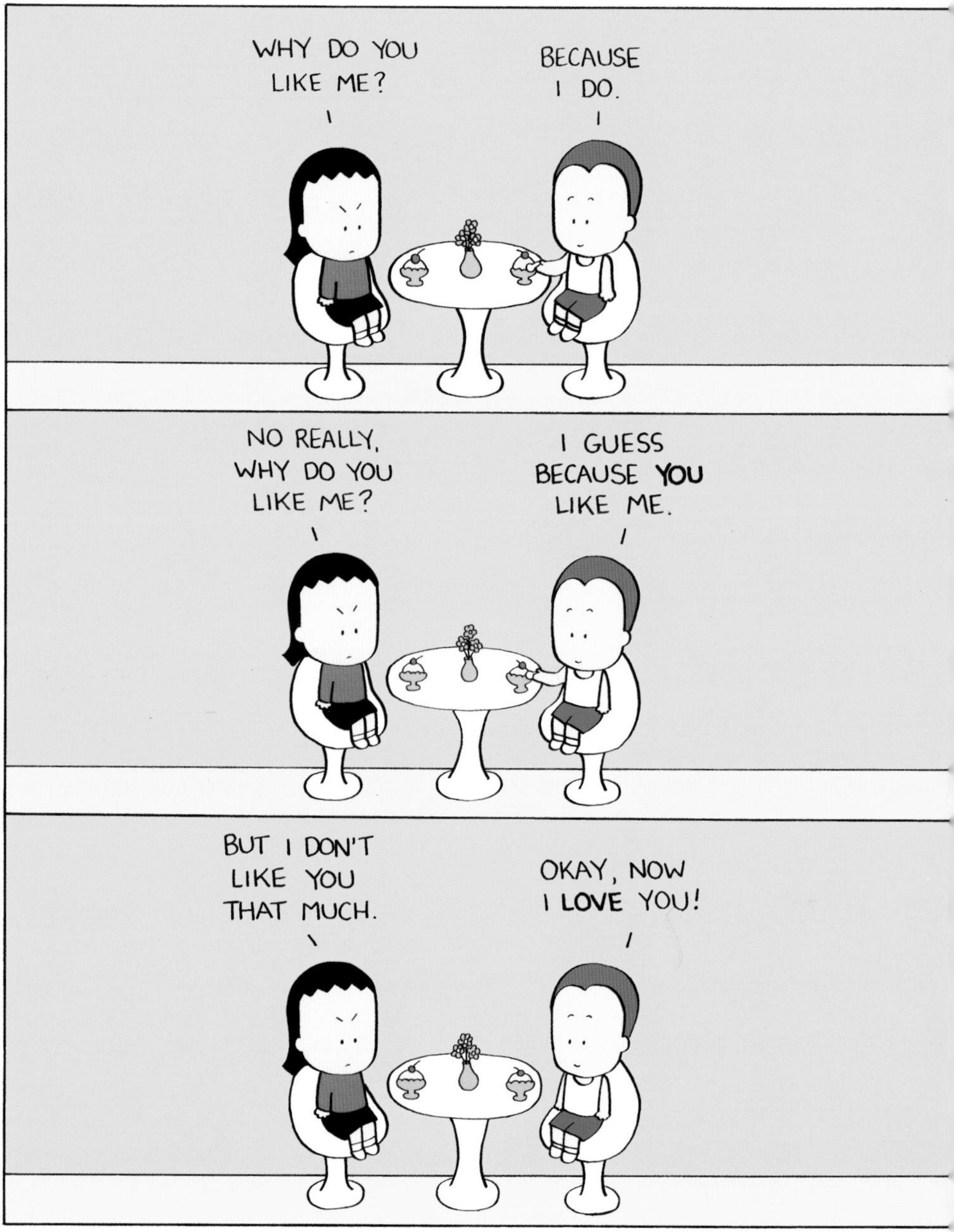
WHY DO YOU LIKE ME?
BECAUSE I DO.
NO REALLY, WHY DO YOU LIKE ME?
I GUESS BECAUSE **YOU** LIKE ME.
BUT I DON'T LIKE YOU THAT MUCH.
OKAY, NOW I **LOVE** YOU!

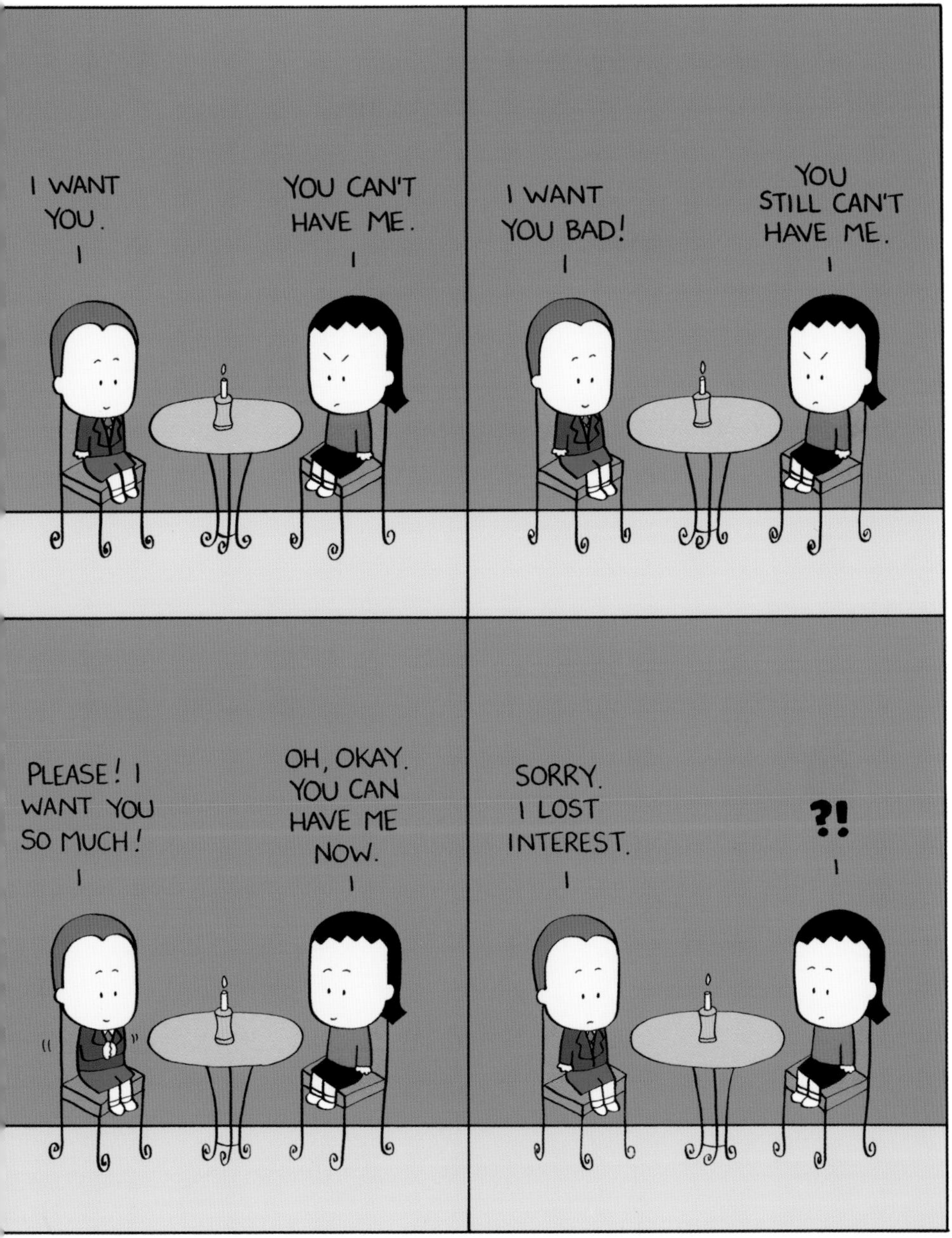
I WANT YOU.
YOU CAN'T HAVE ME.
I WANT YOU BAD!
YOU STILL CAN'T HAVE ME.
PLEASE! I WANT YOU SO MUCH!
OH, OKAY. YOU CAN HAVE ME NOW.
SORRY. I LOST INTEREST.
?!

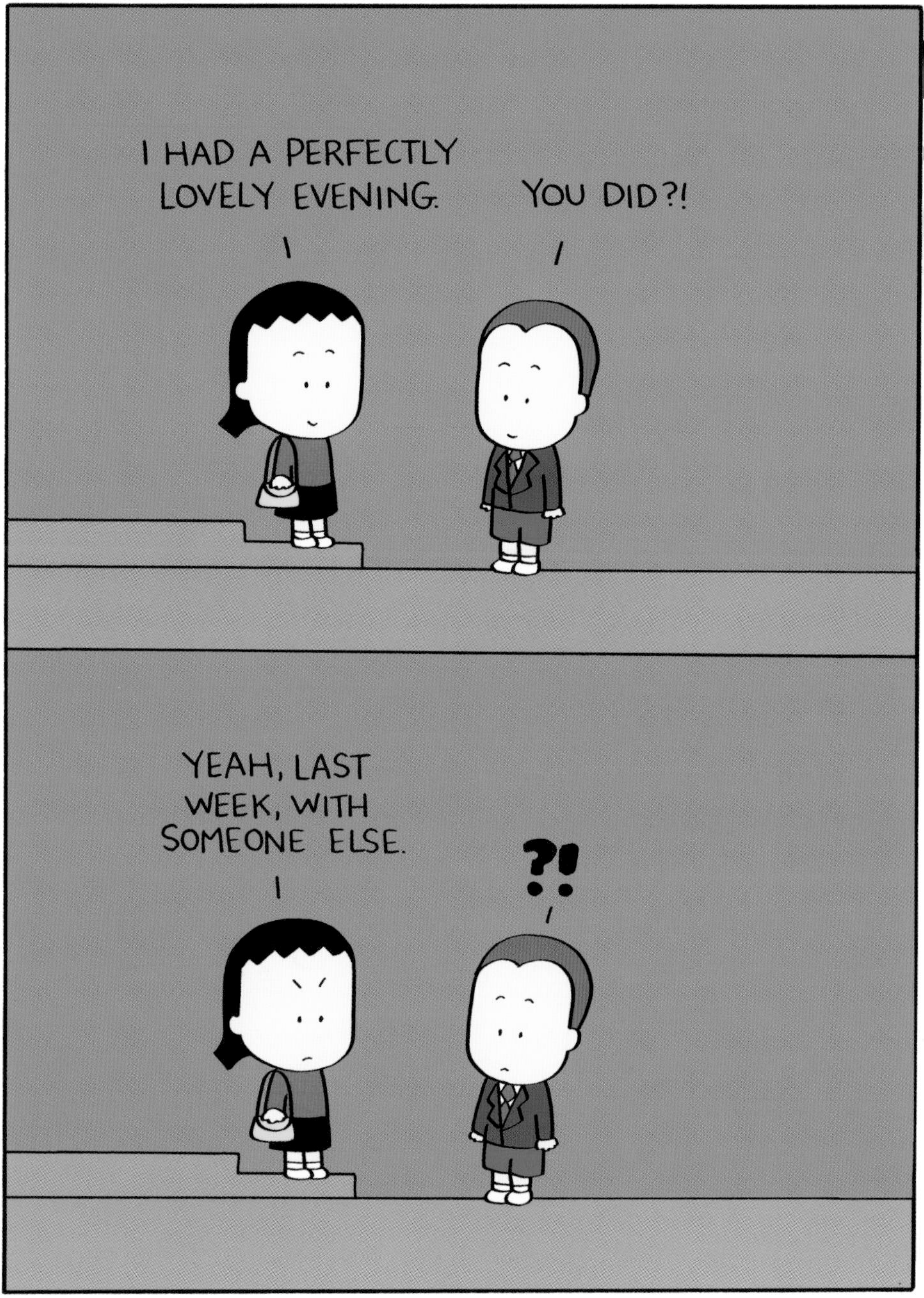
I HAD A PERFECTLY LOVELY EVENING.
YOU DID?!
YEAH, LAST WEEK, WITH SOMEONE ELSE.
?!

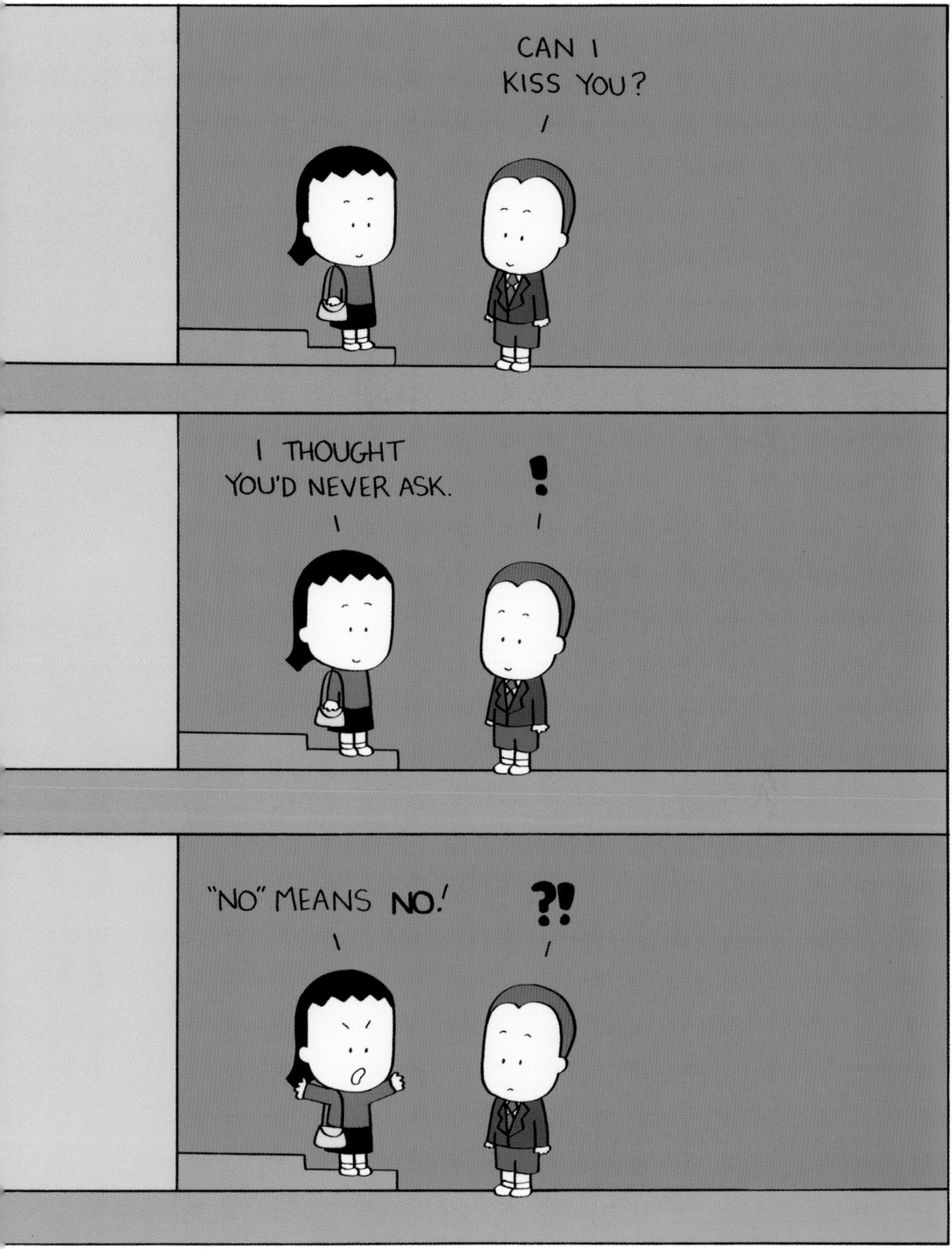
CAN I KISS YOU?
I THOUGHT YOU'D NEVER ASK.
!
"NO" MEANS NO!
?!

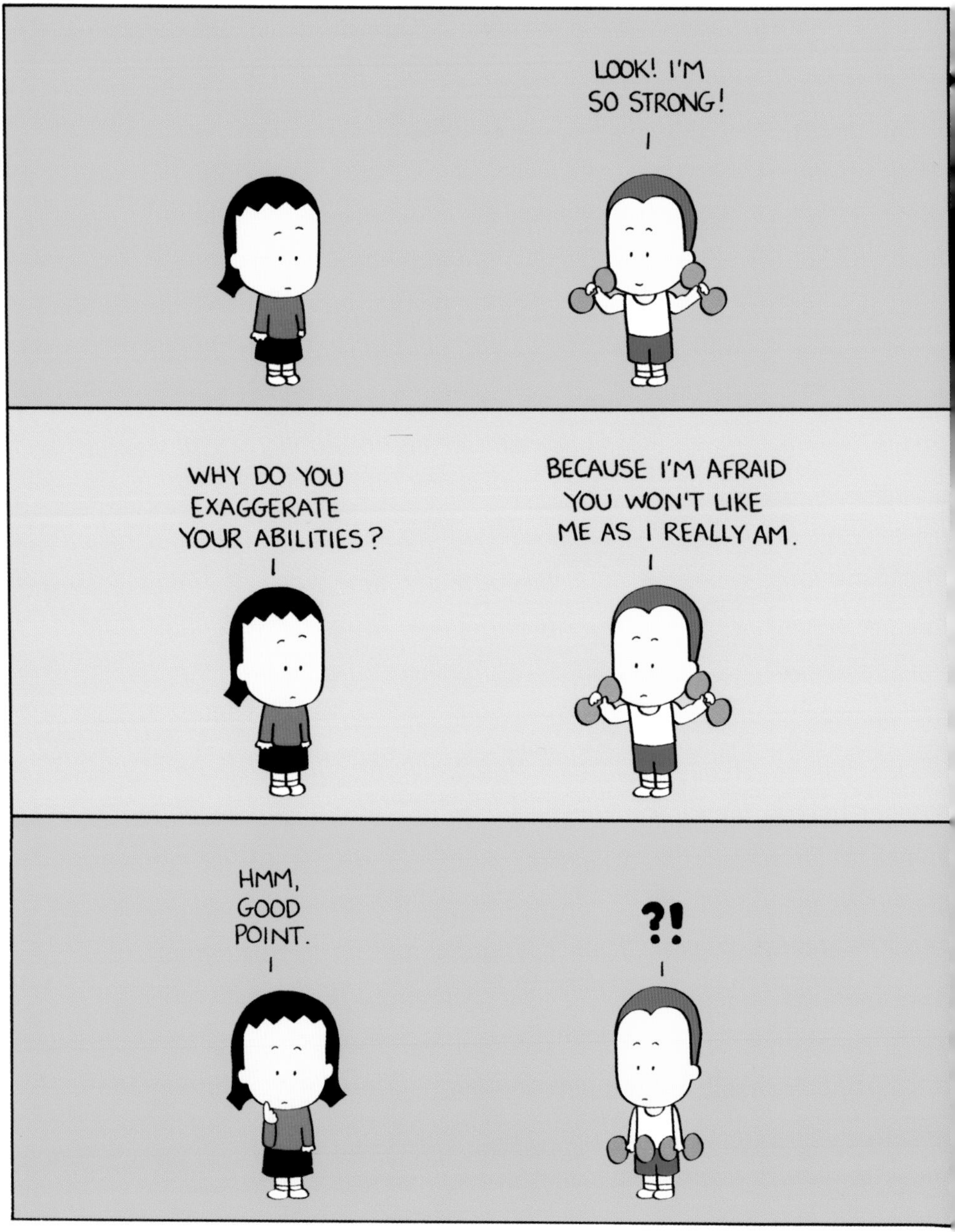
LOOK! I'M SO STRONG!
WHY DO YOU EXAGGERATE YOUR ABILITIES?
BECAUSE I'M AFRAID YOU WON'T LIKE ME AS I REALLY AM.
HMM, GOOD POINT.
?!

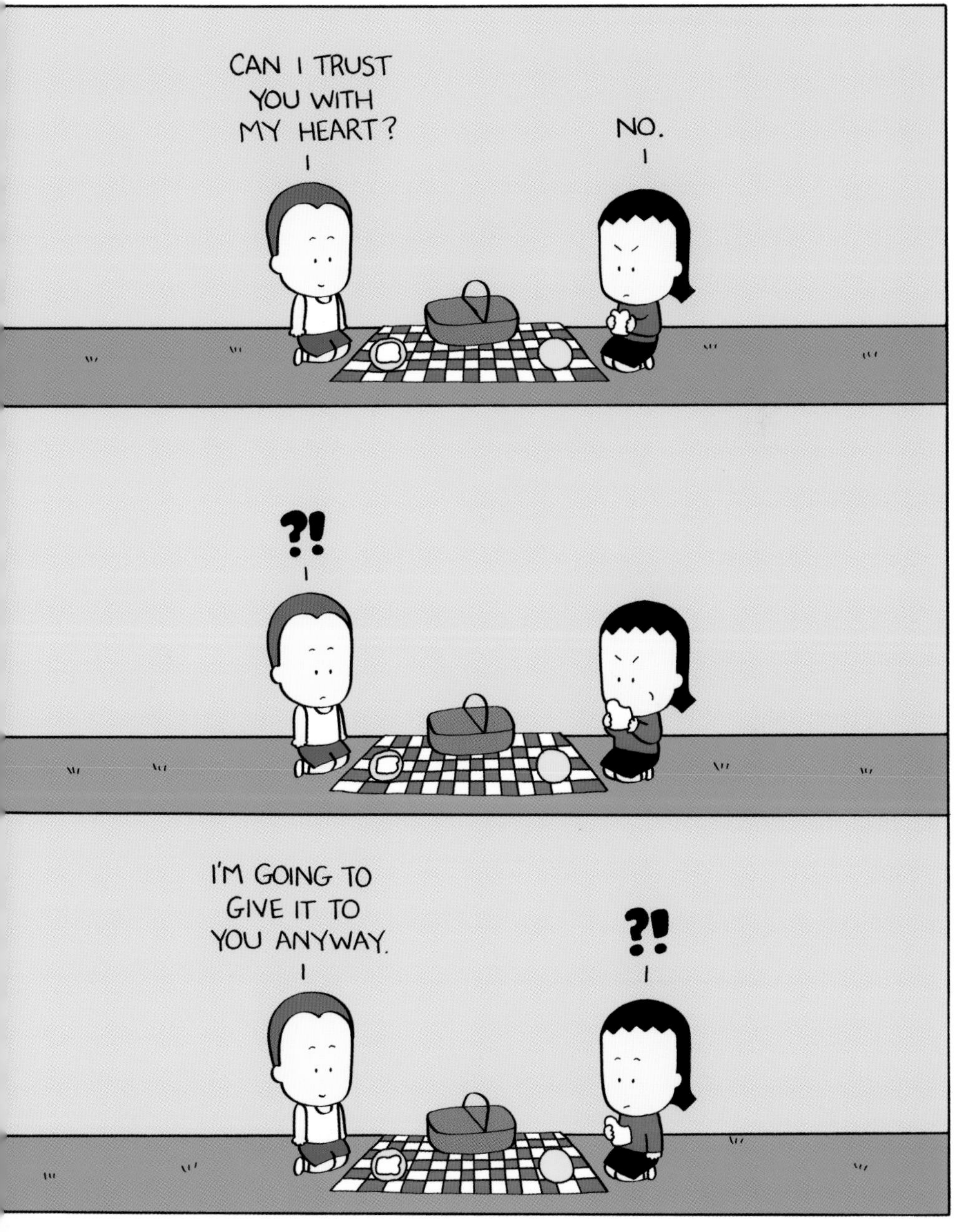
CAN I TRUST YOU WITH MY HEART?
NO.
?!
I'M GOING TO GIVE IT TO YOU ANYWAY.
?!

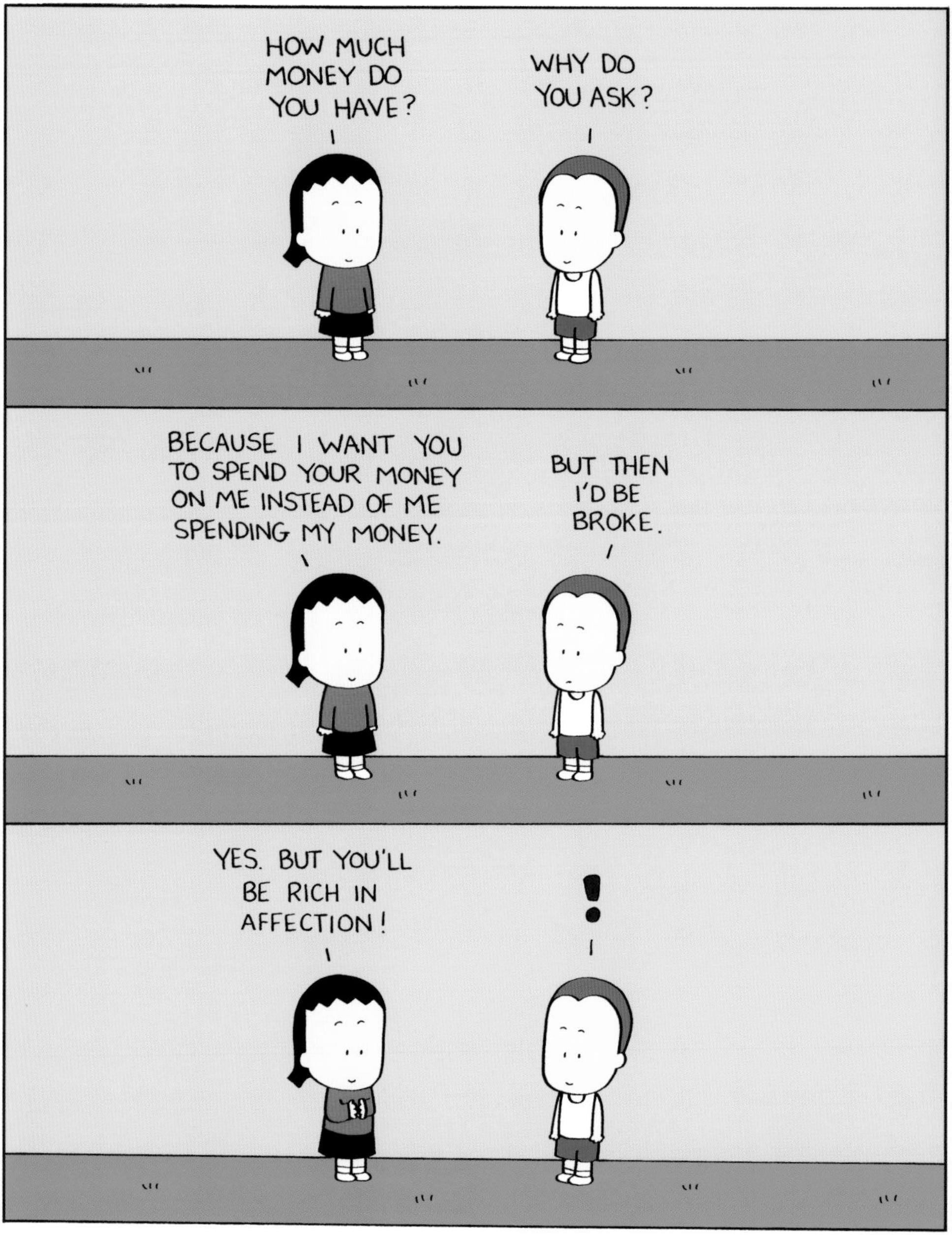
HOW MUCH MONEY DO YOU HAVE?
WHY DO YOU ASK?
BECAUSE I WANT YOU TO SPEND YOUR MONEY ON ME INSTEAD OF ME SPENDING MY MONEY.
BUT THEN I'D BE BROKE.
YES. BUT YOU'LL BE RICH IN AFFECTION!
!

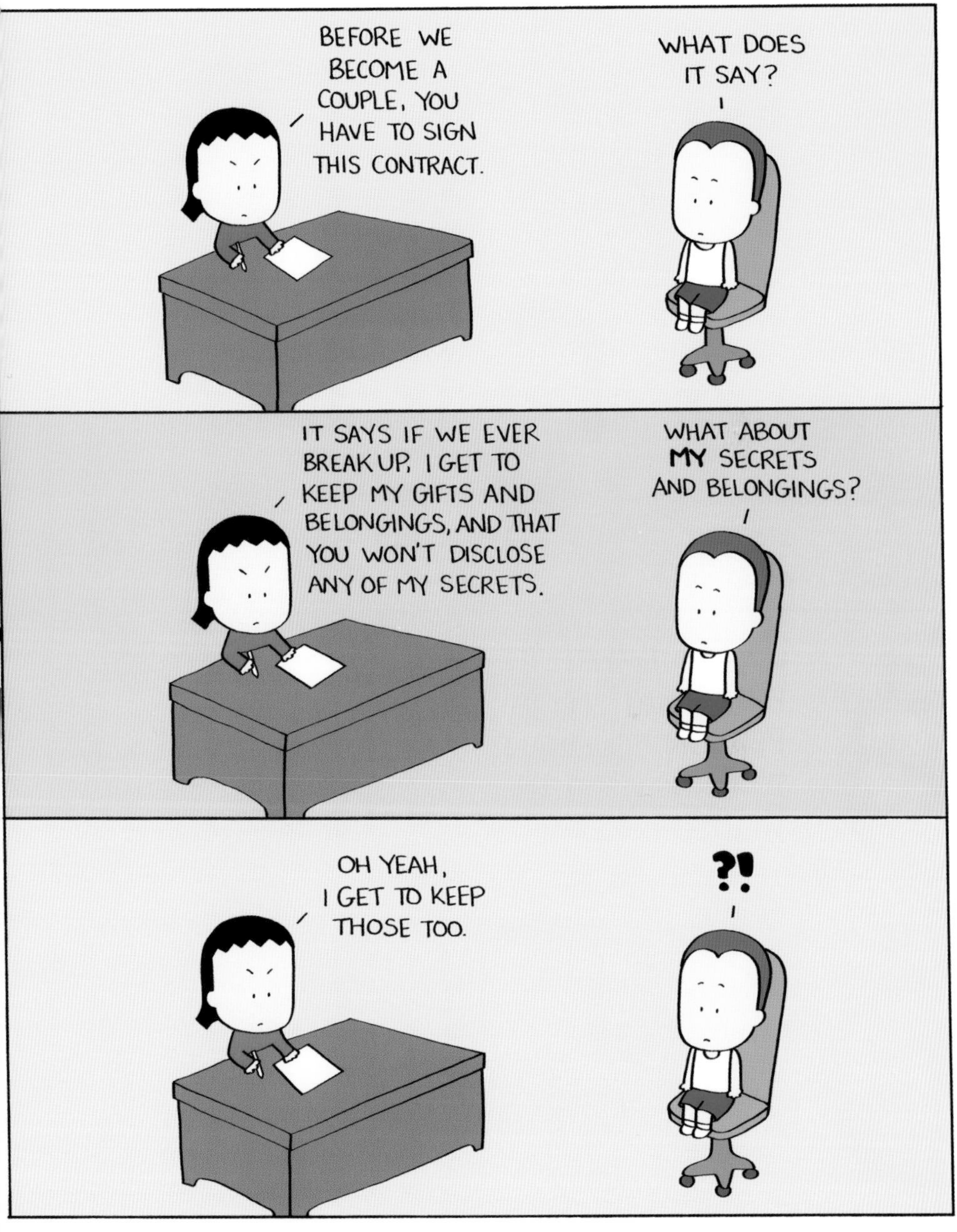
BEFORE WE BECOME A COUPLE, YOU HAVE TO SIGN THIS CONTRACT.
WHAT DOES IT SAY?
IT SAYS IF WE EVER BREAK UP, I GET TO KEEP MY GIFTS AND BELONGINGS, AND THAT YOU WON'T DISCLOSE ANY OF MY SECRETS.
WHAT ABOUT MY SECRETS AND BELONGINGS?
OH YEAH, I GET TO KEEP THOSE TOO.
?!

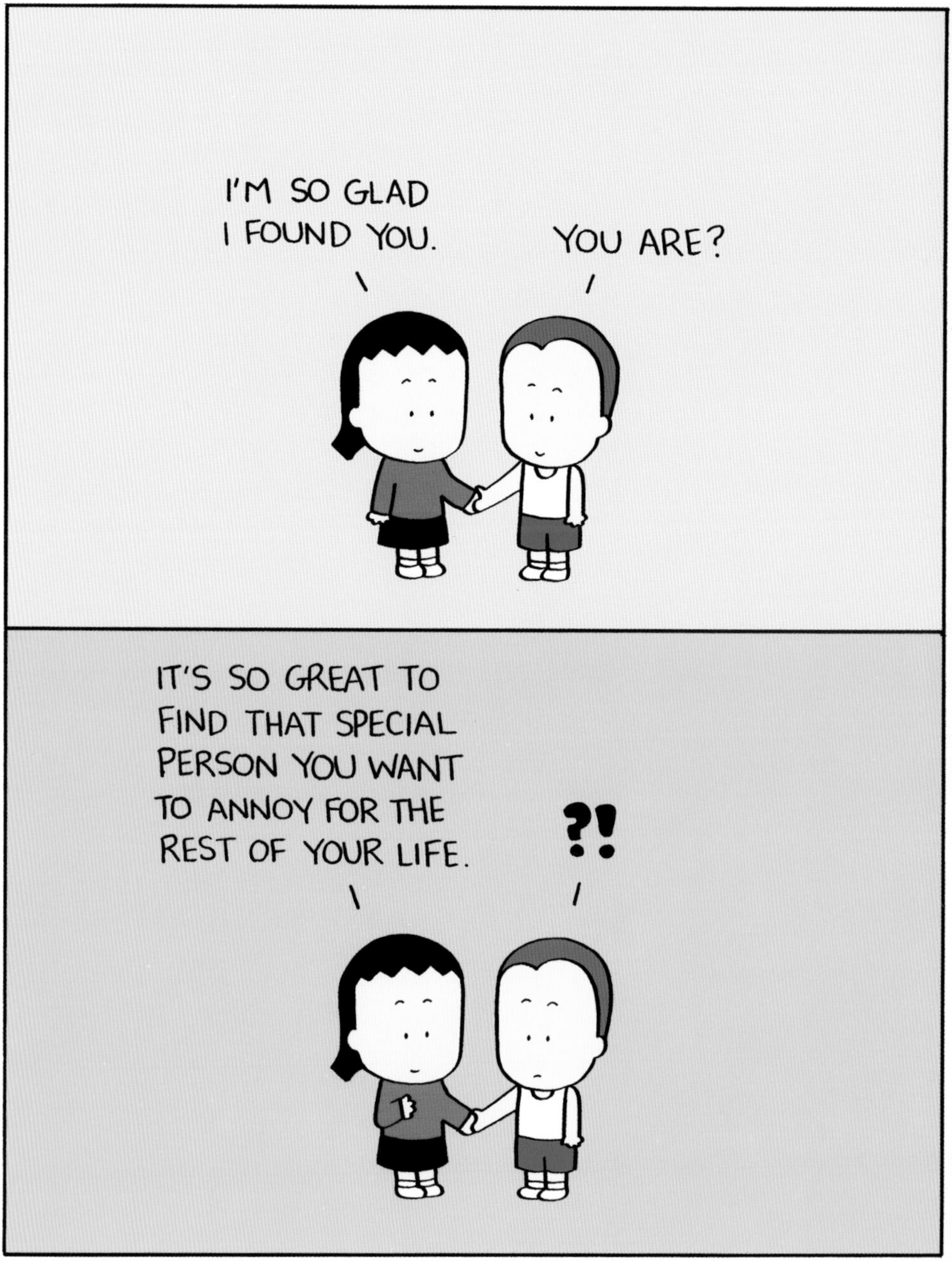
I'M SO GLAD I FOUND YOU.
YOU ARE?
IT'S SO GREAT TO FIND THAT SPECIAL PERSON YOU WANT TO ANNOY FOR THE REST OF YOUR LIFE.
?!

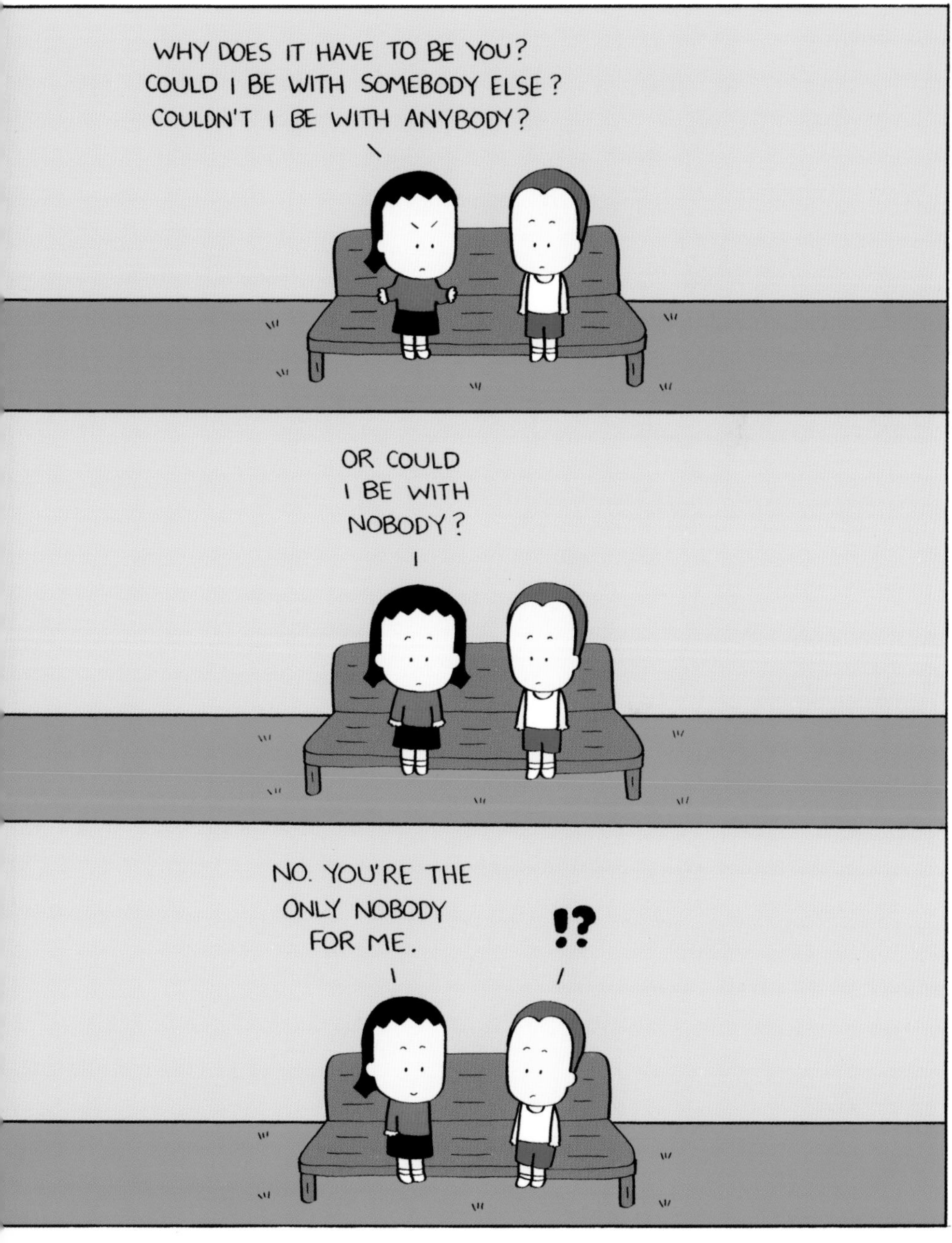
WHY DOES IT HAVE TO BE YOU? COULD I BE WITH SOMEBODY ELSE? COULDN'T I BE WITH ANYBODY?
OR COULD I BE WITH NOBODY?
NO. YOU'RE THE ONLY NOBODY FOR ME.
!?

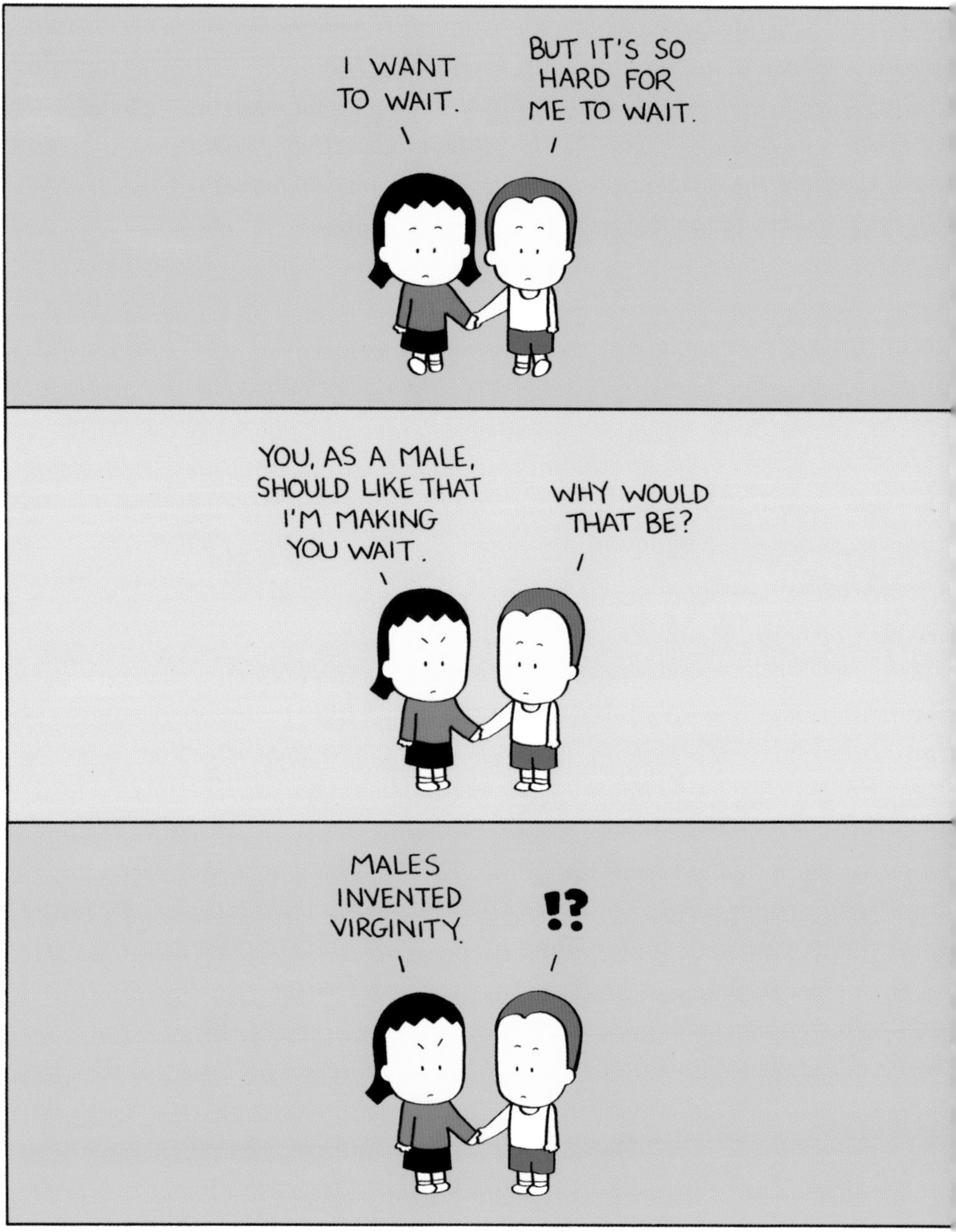
I WANT TO WAIT.
BUT IT'S SO HARD FOR ME TO WAIT.
YOU, AS A MALE, SHOULD LIKE THAT I'M MAKING YOU WAIT.
WHY WOULD THAT BE?
MALES INVENTED VIRGINITY.
!?

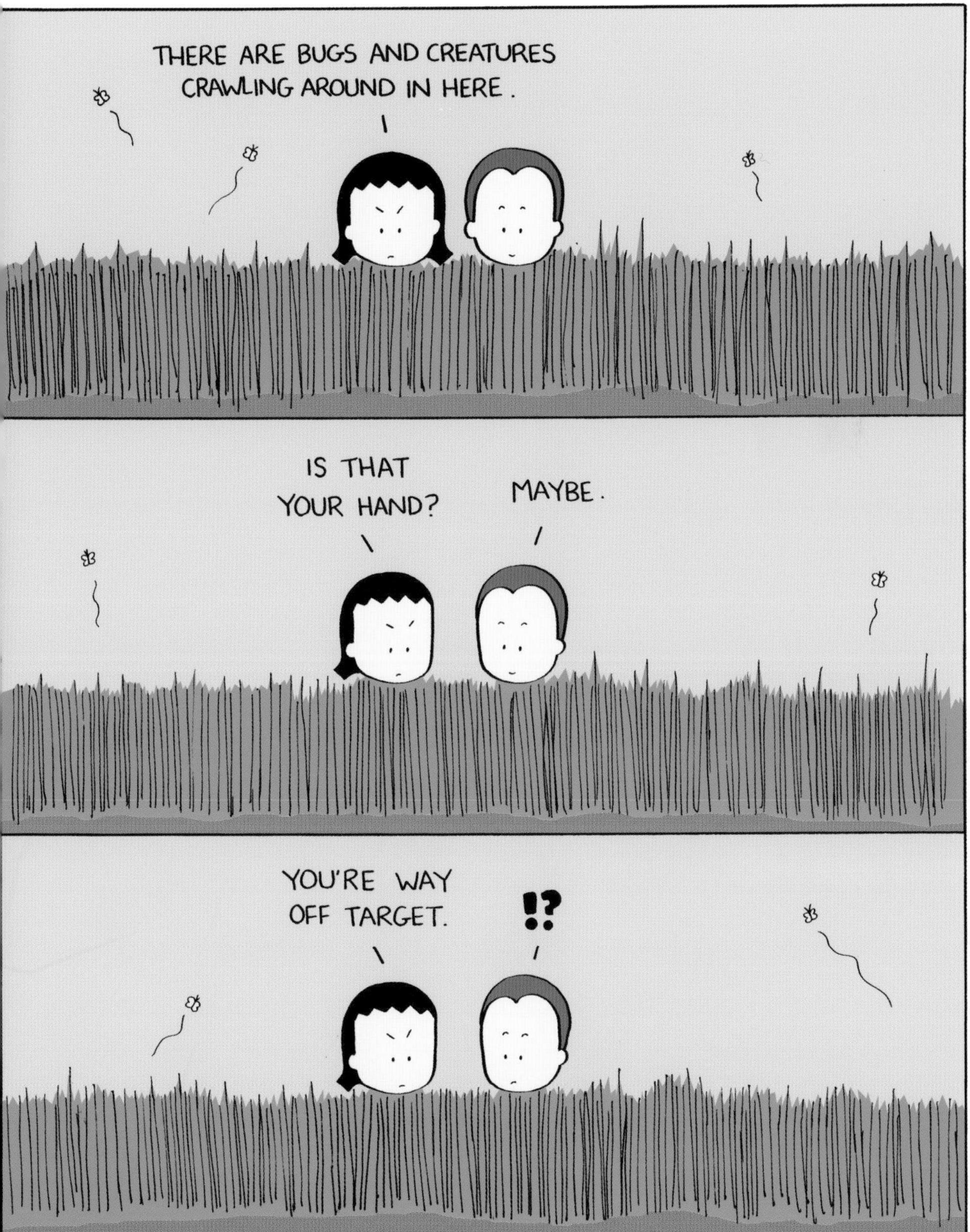
THERE ARE BUGS AND CREATURES CRAWLING AROUND IN HERE.
IS THAT YOUR HAND?
MAYBE.
YOU'RE WAY OFF TARGET.
!?

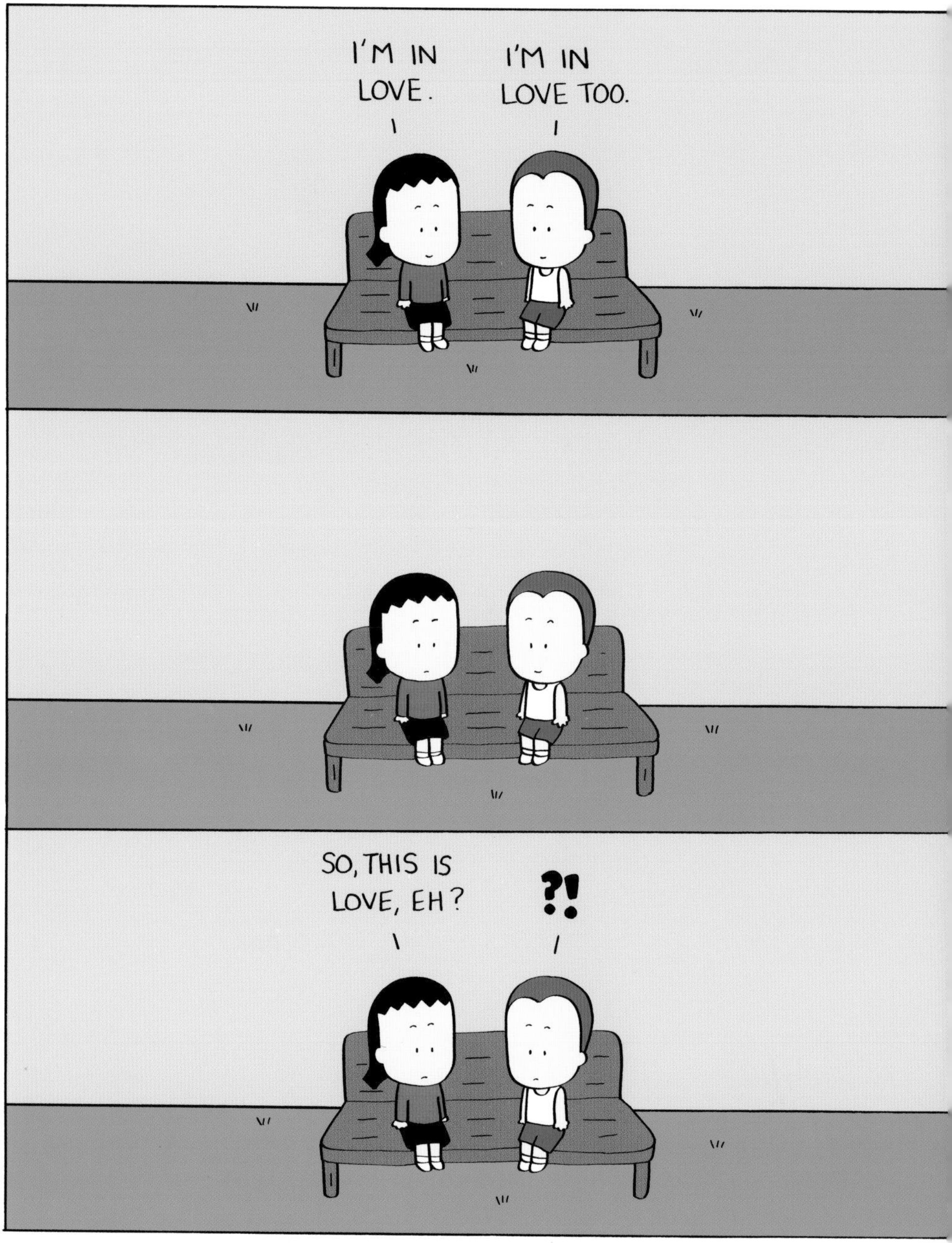
I'M IN LOVE.
I'M IN LOVE TOO.
SO, THIS IS LOVE, EH?
?!

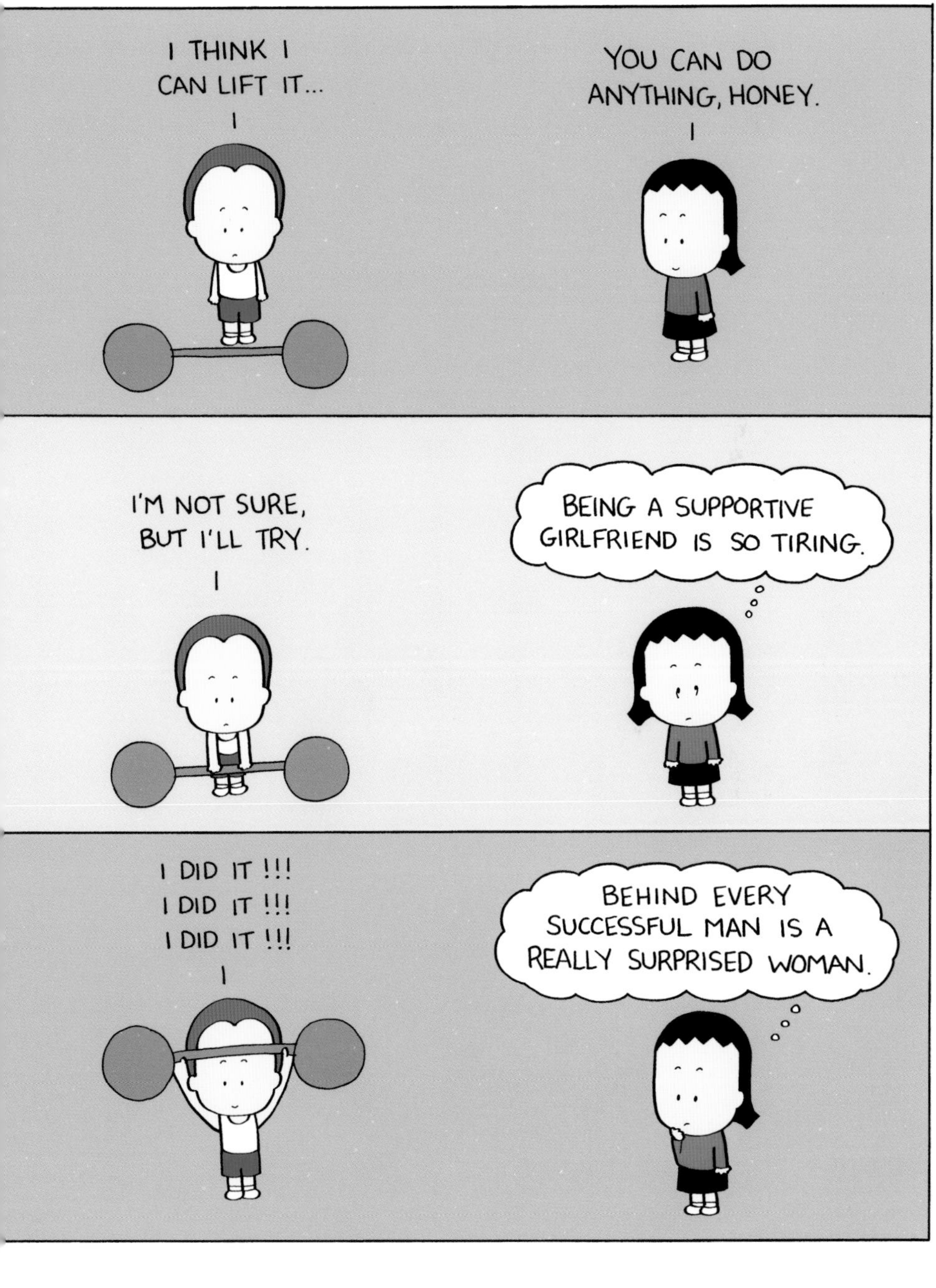
I THINK I CAN LIFT IT...
YOU CAN DO ANYTHING, HONEY.
I'M NOT SURE, BUT I'LL TRY.
BEING A SUPPORTIVE GIRLFRIEND IS SO TIRING.
I DID IT !!! I DID IT !!! I DID IT !!!
BEHIND EVERY SUCCESSFUL MAN IS A REALLY SURPRISED WOMAN.

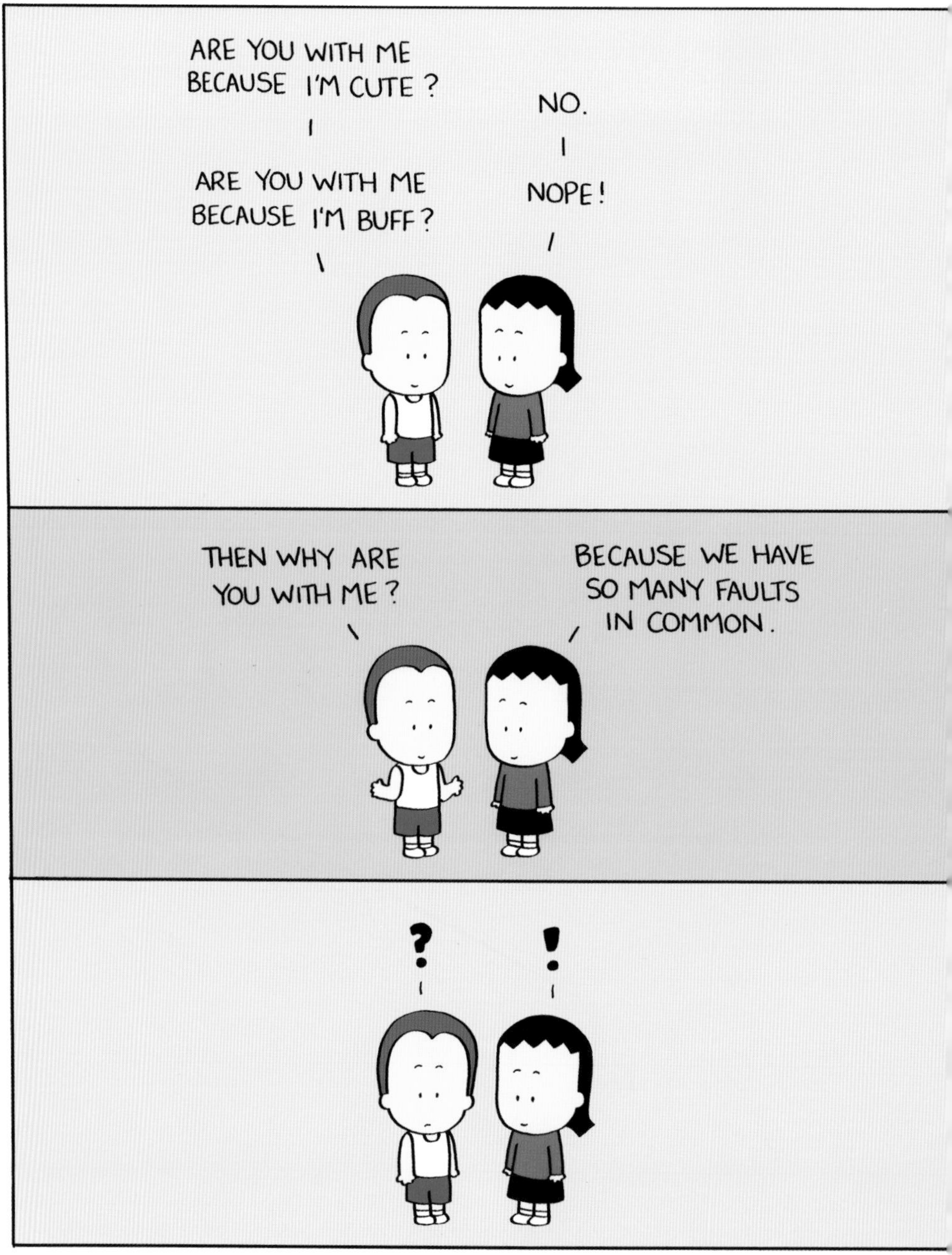
ARE YOU WITH ME BECAUSE I'M CUTE?
NO.
ARE YOU WITH ME BECAUSE I'M BUFF?
NOPE!
THEN WHY ARE YOU WITH ME?
BECAUSE WE HAVE SO MANY FAULTS IN COMMON.
?
!

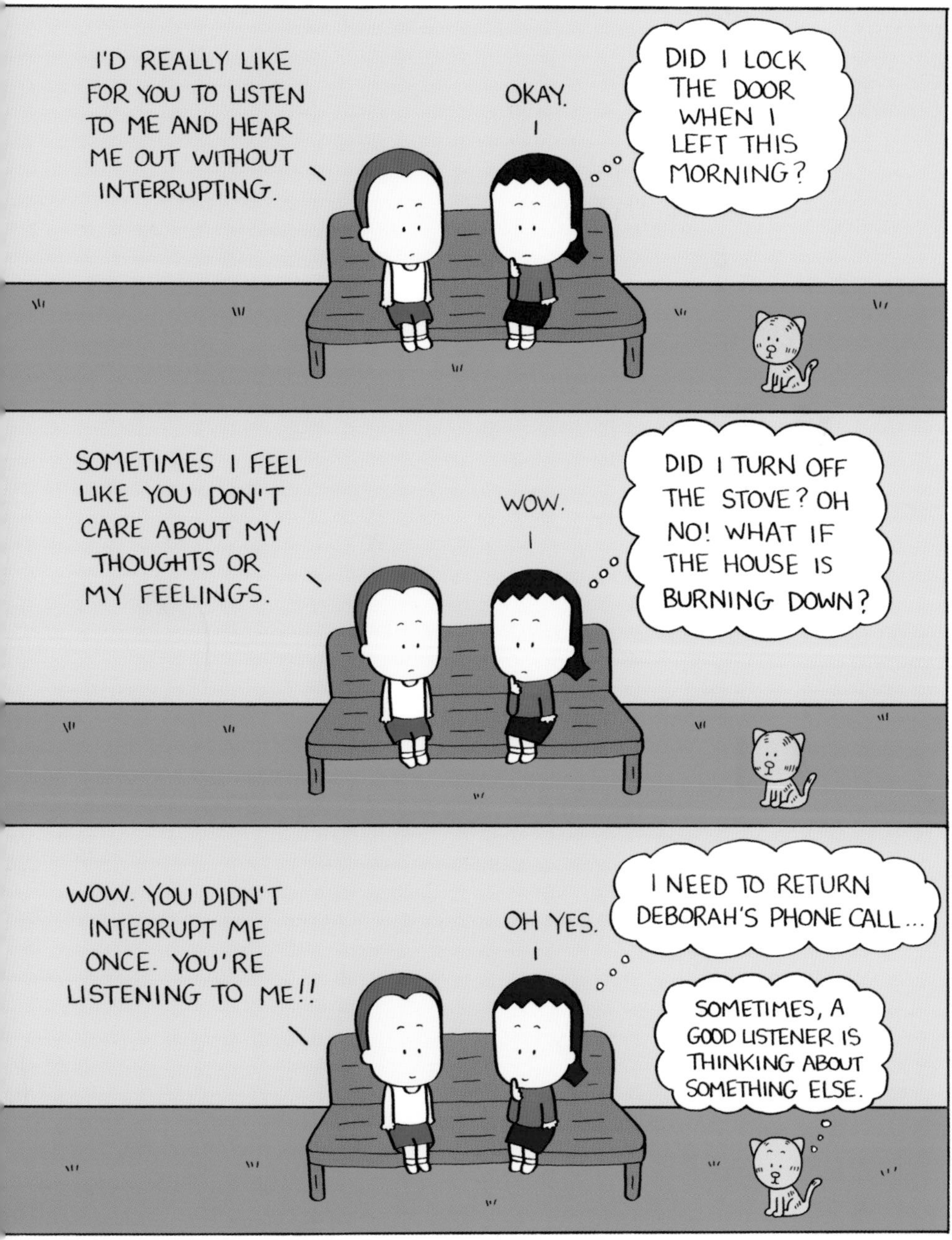
I'D REALLY LIKE FOR YOU TO LISTEN TO ME AND HEAR ME OUT WITHOUT INTERRUPTING.
OKAY.
DID I LOCK THE DOOR WHEN I LEFT THIS MORNING?
SOMETIMES I FEEL LIKE YOU DON'T CARE ABOUT MY THOUGHTS OR MY FEELINGS.
WOW.
DID I TURN OFF THE STOVE? OH NO! WHAT IF THE HOUSE IS BURNING DOWN?
WOW. YOU DIDN'T INTERRUPT ME ONCE. YOU'RE LISTENING TO ME!!
OH YES.
I NEED TO RETURN DEBORAH'S PHONE CALL...
SOMETIMES, A GOOD LISTENER IS THINKING ABOUT SOMETHING ELSE.

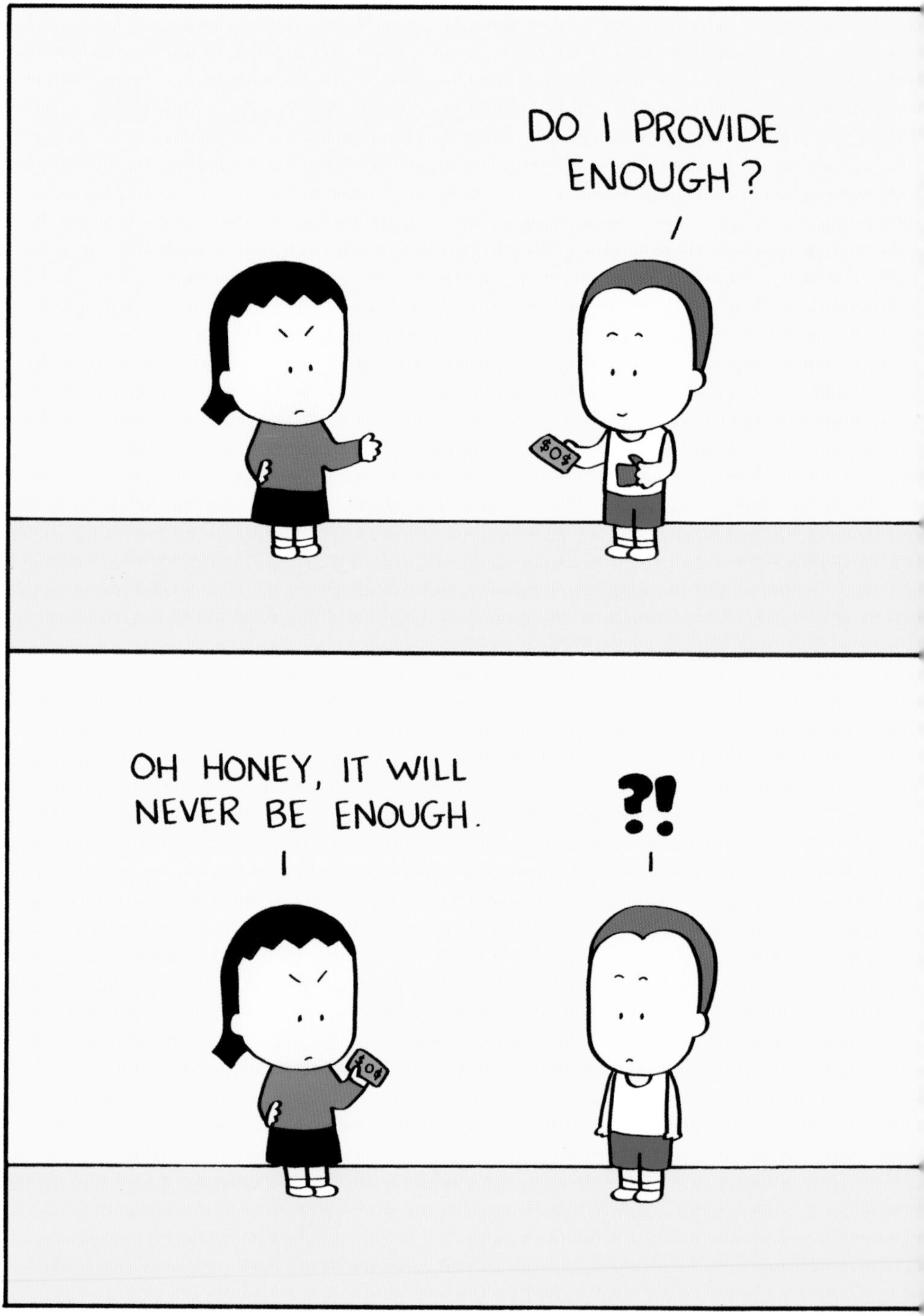
DO I PROVIDE ENOUGH?
0
OH HONEY, IT WILL NEVER BE ENOUGH.
?!
0

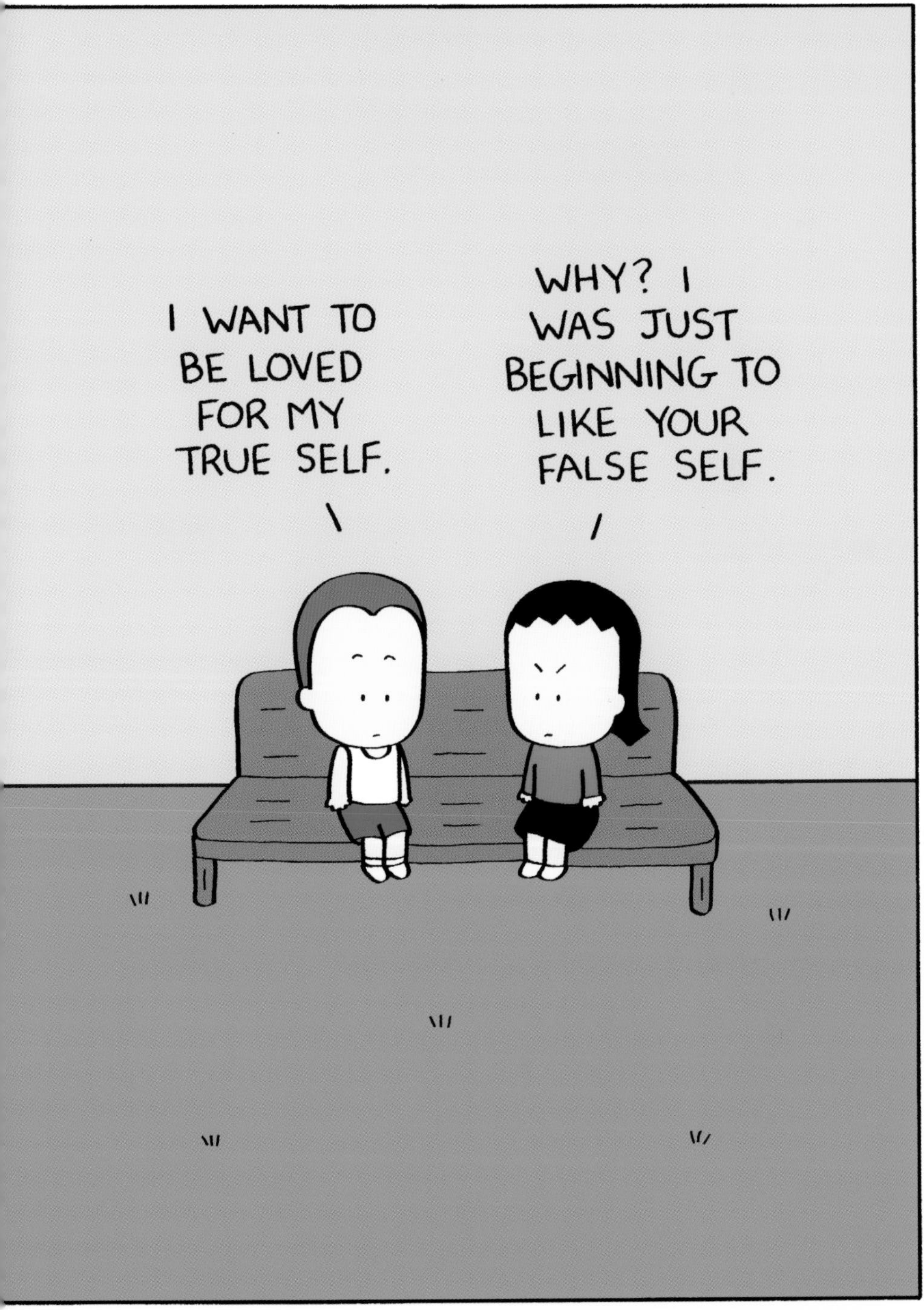
I WANT TO BE LOVED FOR MY TRUE SELF.
WHY? I WAS JUST BEGINNING TO LIKE YOUR FALSE SELF.

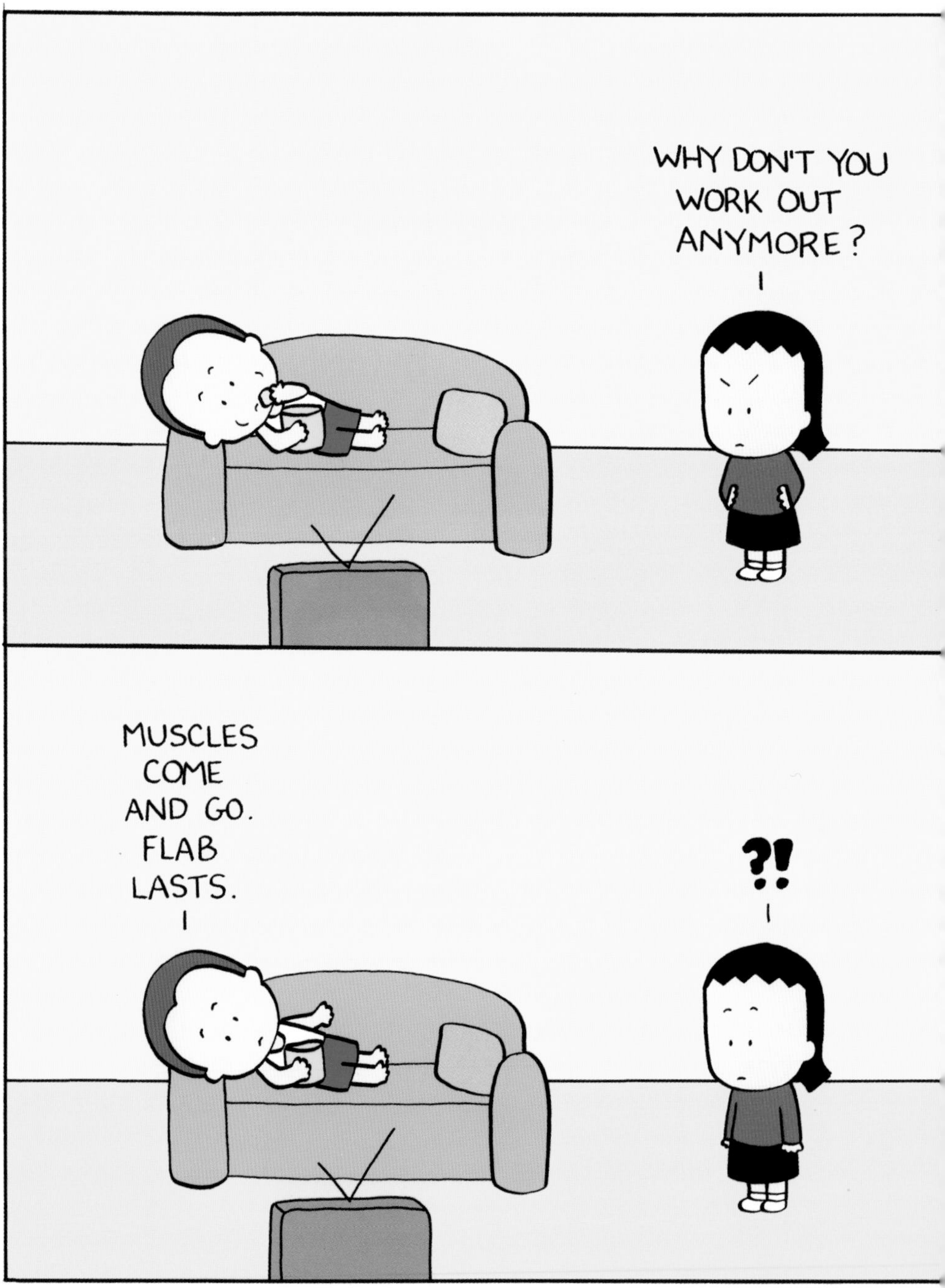
WHY DON'T YOU WORK OUT ANYMORE?
MUSCLES COME AND GO. FLAB LASTS.
?!

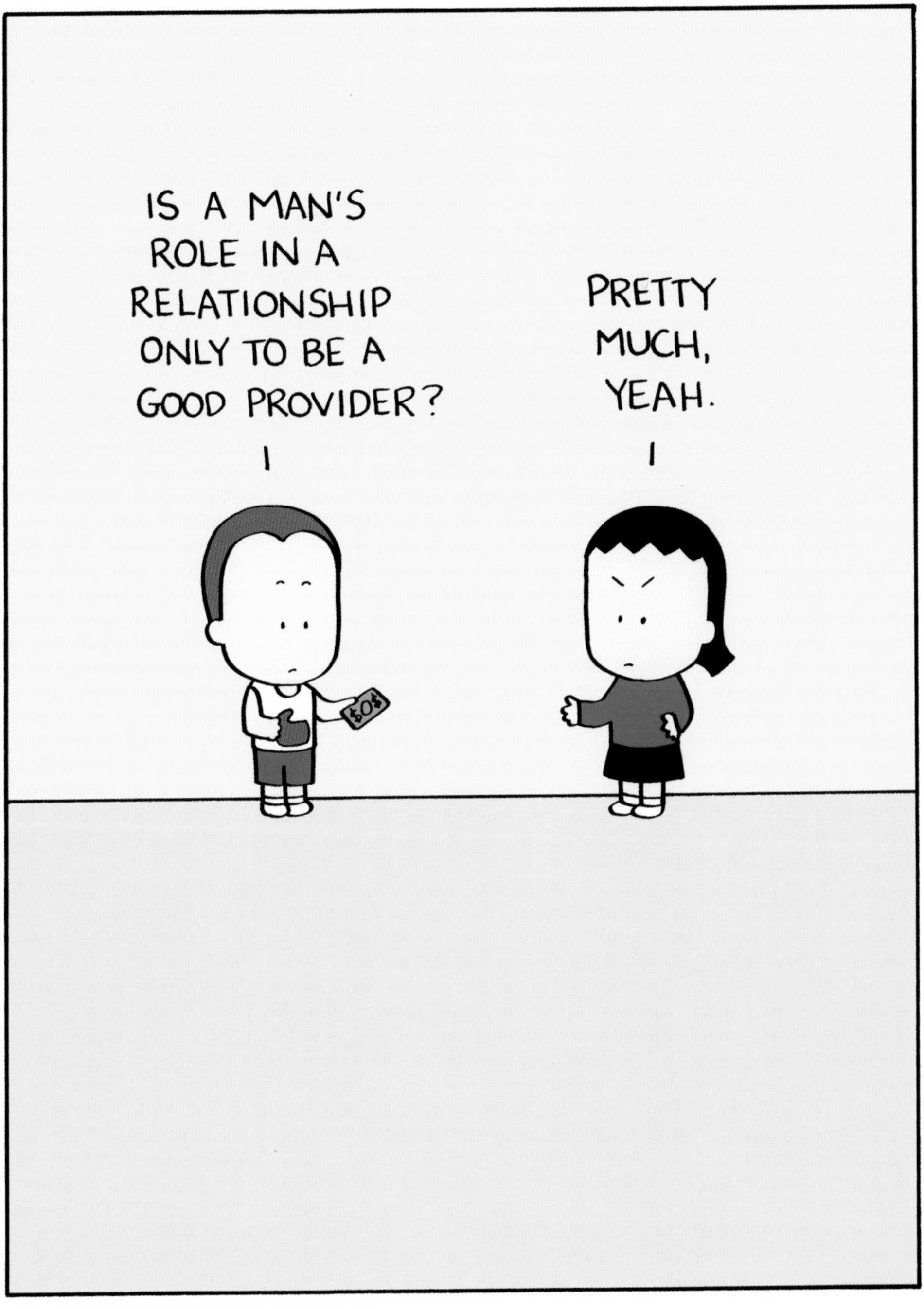
IS A MAN'S ROLE IN A RELATIONSHIP ONLY TO BE A GOOD PROVIDER?
PRETTY MUCH, YEAH.
0

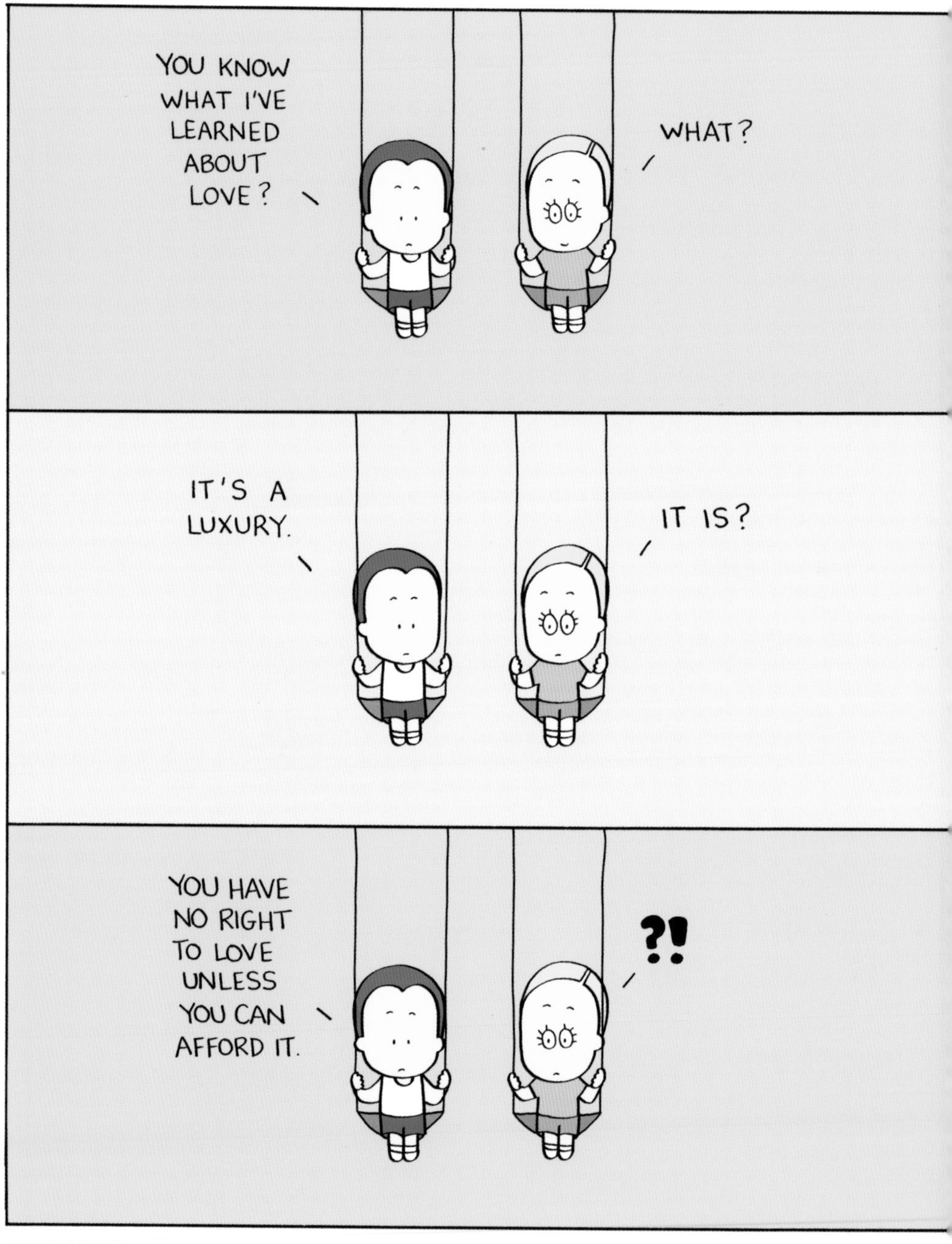
YOU KNOW WHAT I'VE LEARNED ABOUT LOVE?
WHAT?
IT'S A LUXURY.
IT IS?
YOU HAVE NO RIGHT TO LOVE UNLESS YOU CAN AFFORD IT.
?!

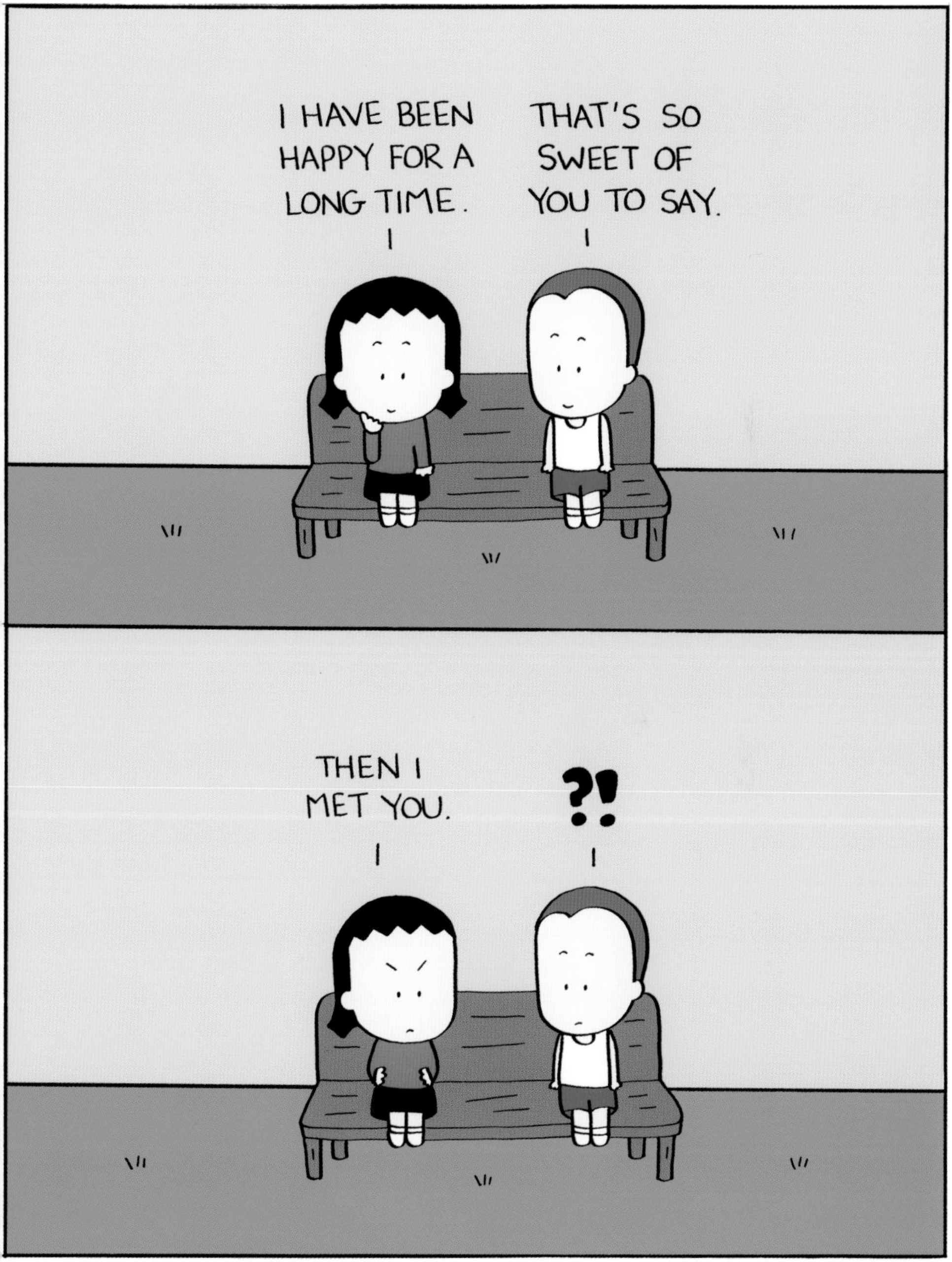
I HAVE BEEN HAPPY FOR A LONG TIME.
THAT'S SO SWEET OF YOU TO SAY.
THEN I MET YOU.
?!

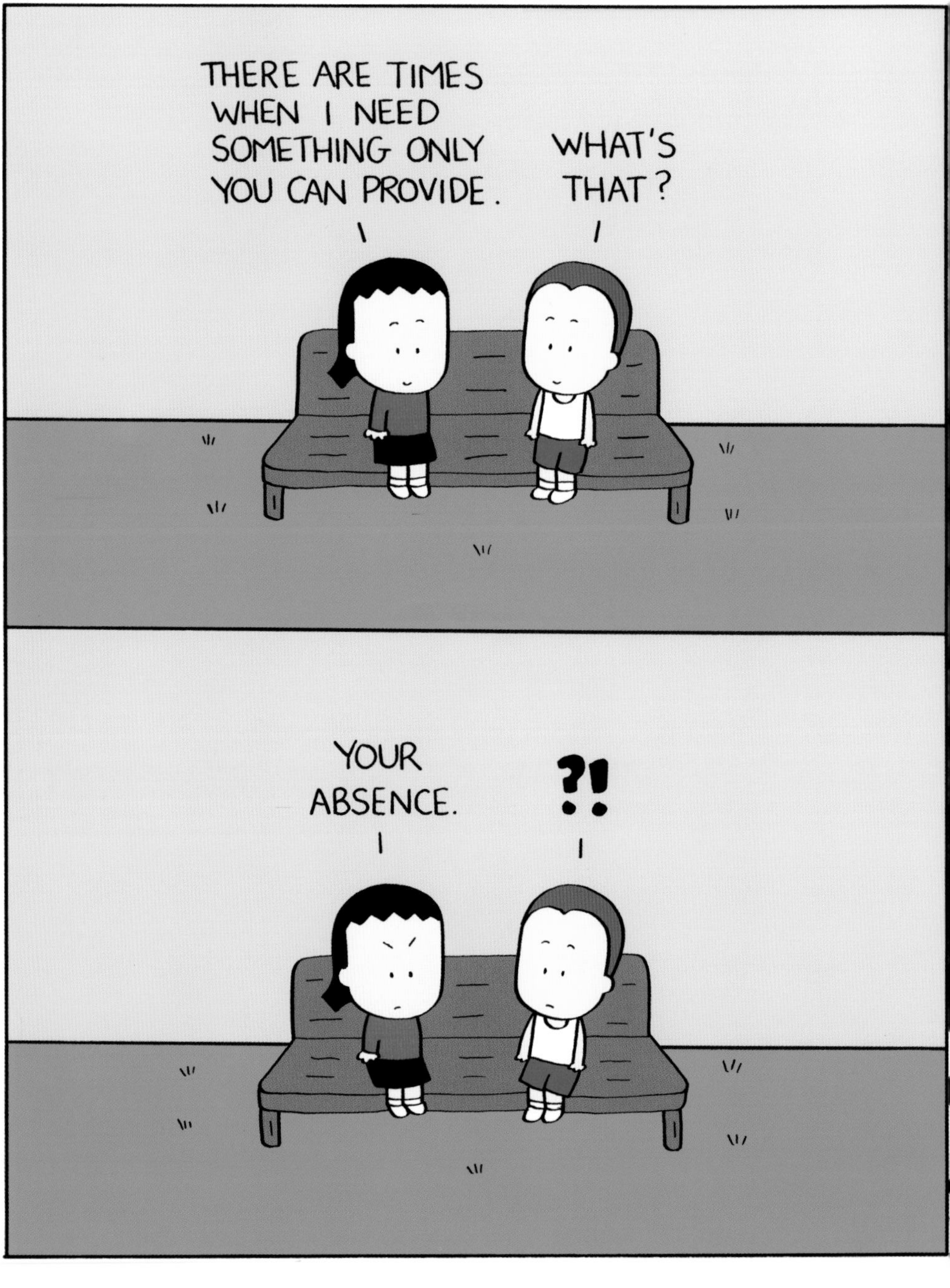
THERE ARE TIMES WHEN I NEED SOMETHING ONLY YOU CAN PROVIDE.
WHAT'S THAT?
YOUR ABSENCE.
?!

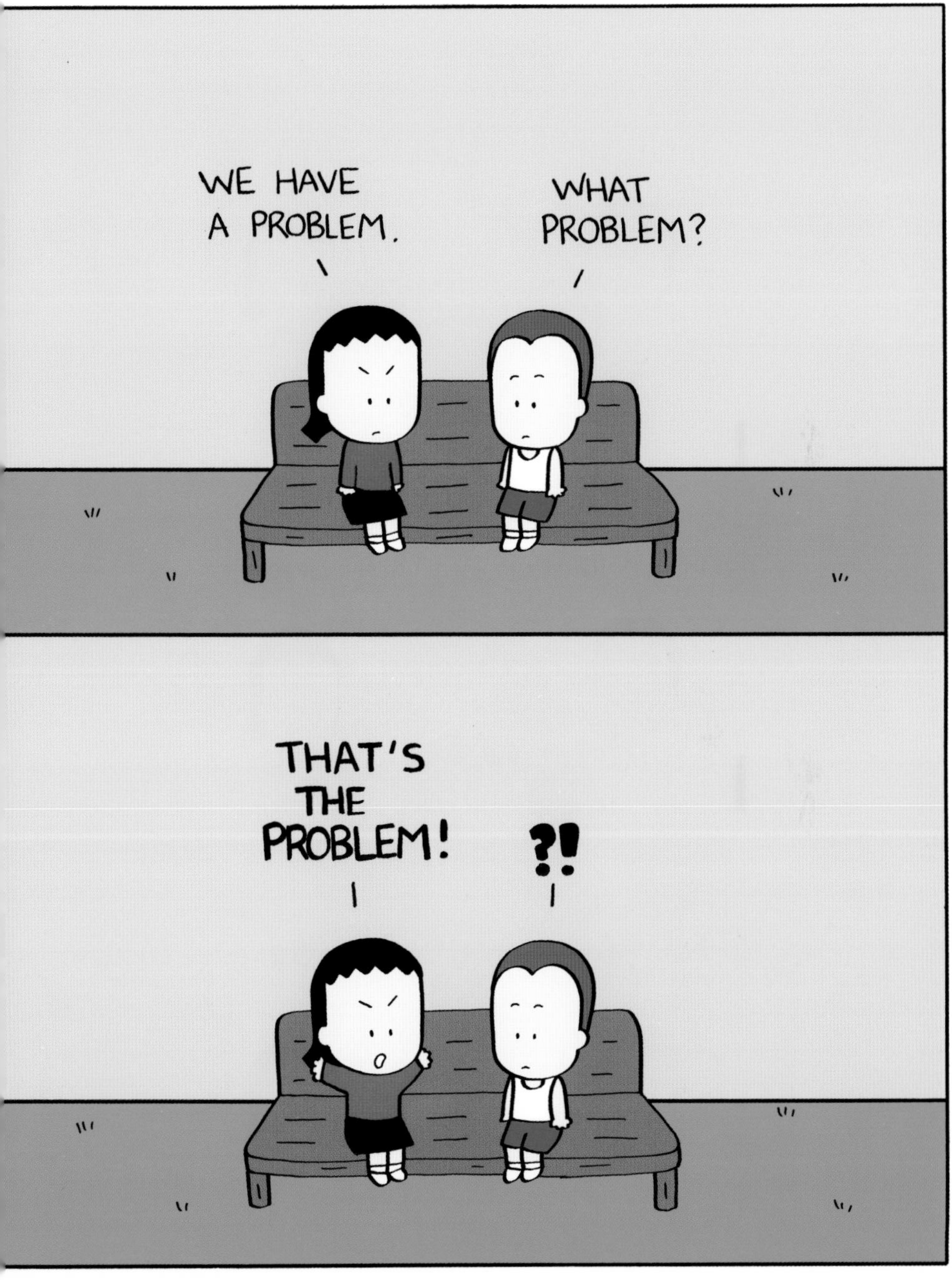
WE HAVE A PROBLEM.
WHAT PROBLEM?
THAT'S THE PROBLEM!
?!

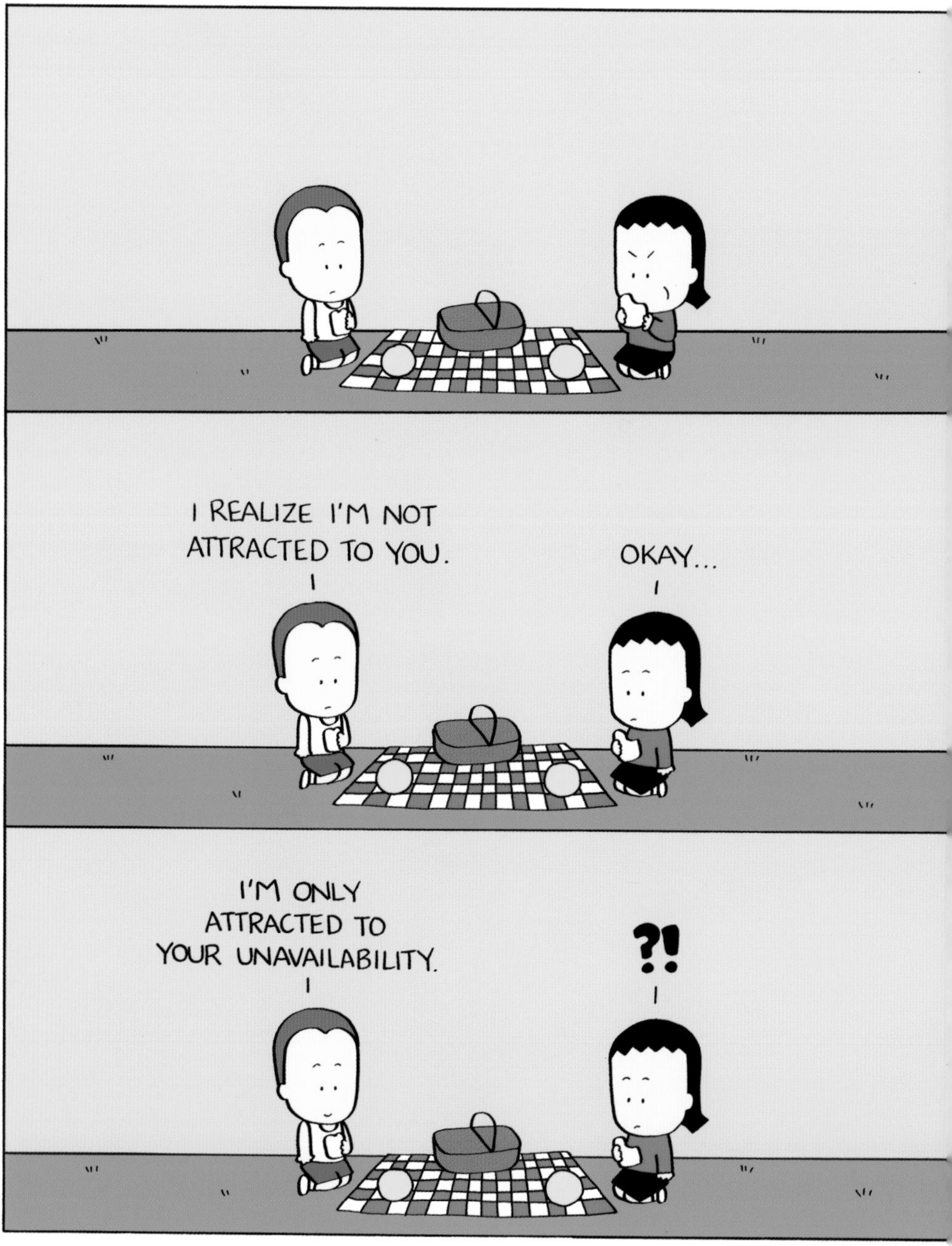
I REALIZE I'M NOT ATTRACTED TO YOU.
OKAY...
I'M ONLY ATTRACTED TO YOUR UNAVAILABILITY.
?!

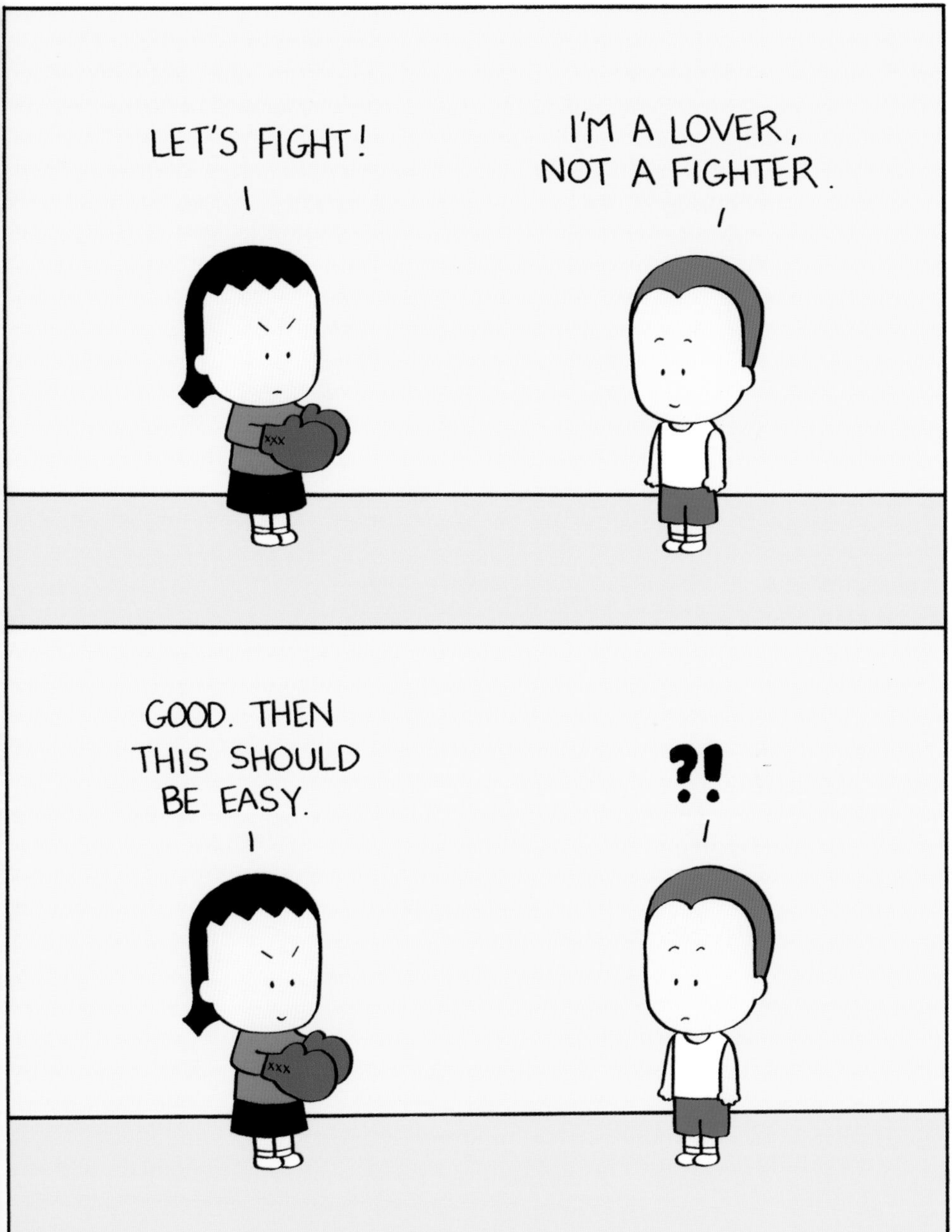
LET'S FIGHT!
I'M A LOVER, NOT A FIGHTER.
XXX
GOOD. THEN THIS SHOULD BE EASY.
?!
XXX

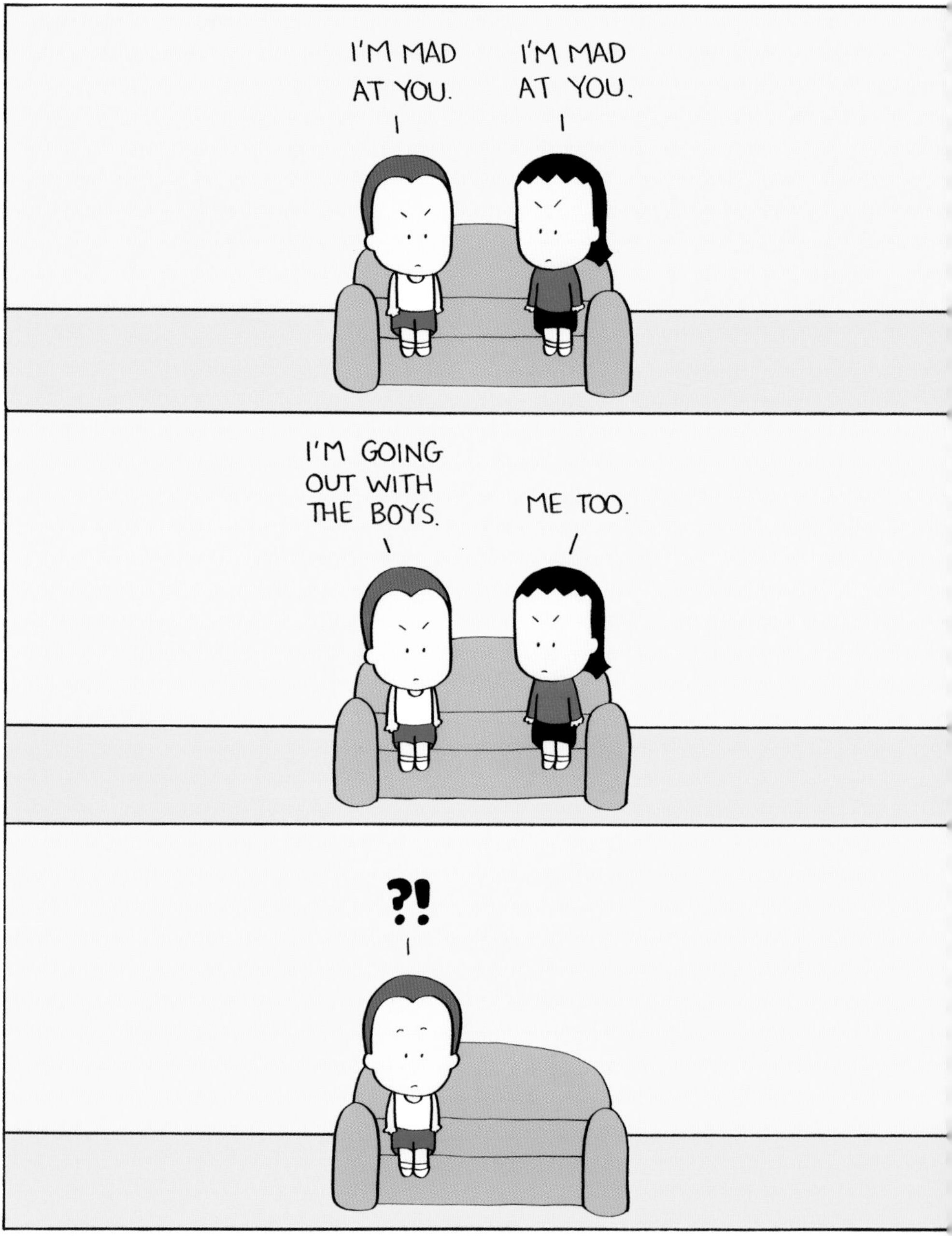
I'M MAD AT YOU.
I'M MAD AT YOU.
I'M GOING OUT WITH THE BOYS.
ME TOO.
?!

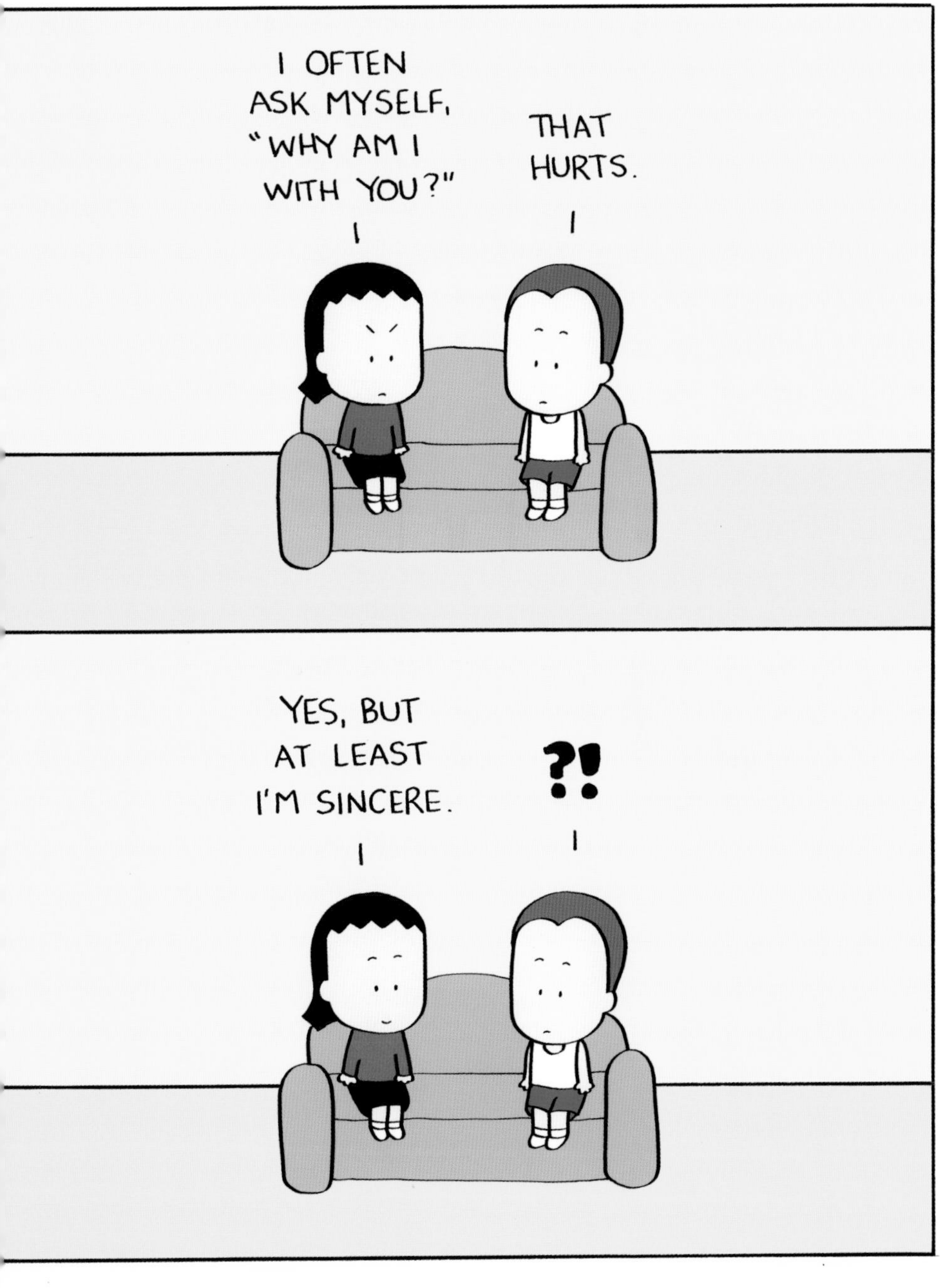
I OFTEN ASK MYSELF, "WHY AM I WITH YOU?"
THAT HURTS.
YES, BUT AT LEAST I'M SINCERE.
?!

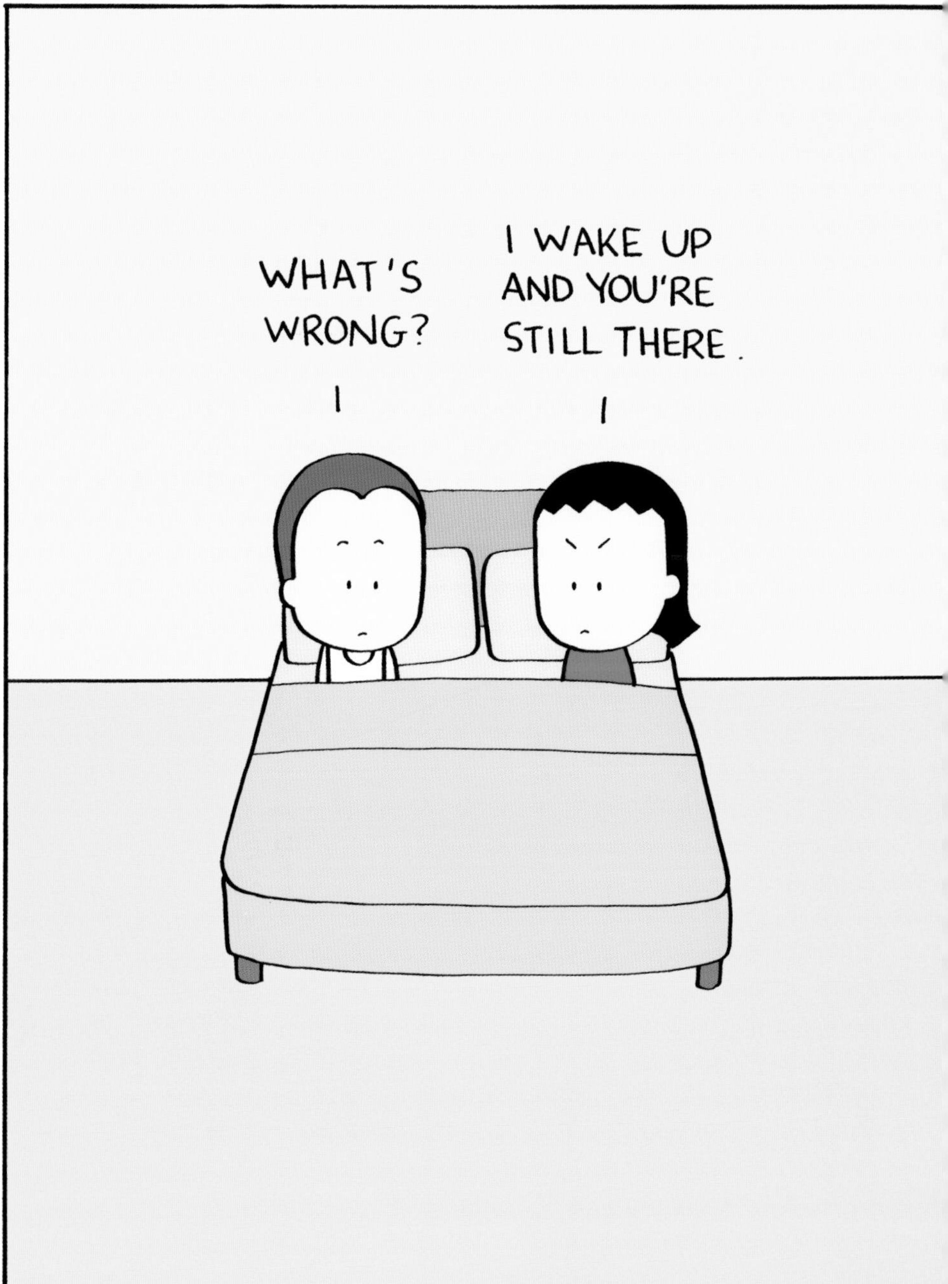
WHAT'S WRONG?
I WAKE UP AND YOU'RE STILL THERE.

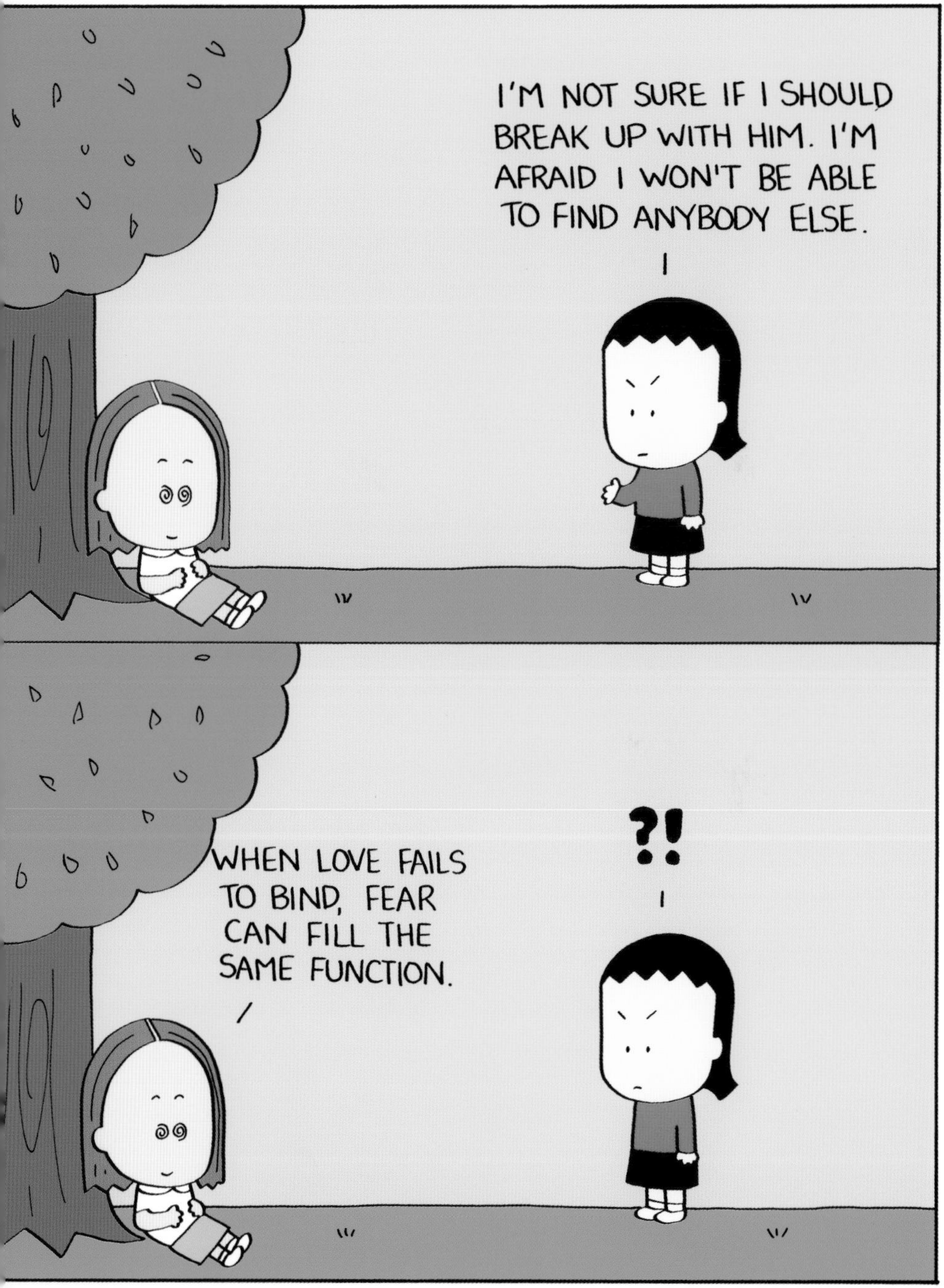
I'M NOT SURE IF I SHOULD BREAK UP WITH HIM. I'M AFRAID I WON'T BE ABLE TO FIND ANYBODY ELSE.
?!
WHEN LOVE FAILS TO BIND, FEAR CAN FILL THE SAME FUNCTION.

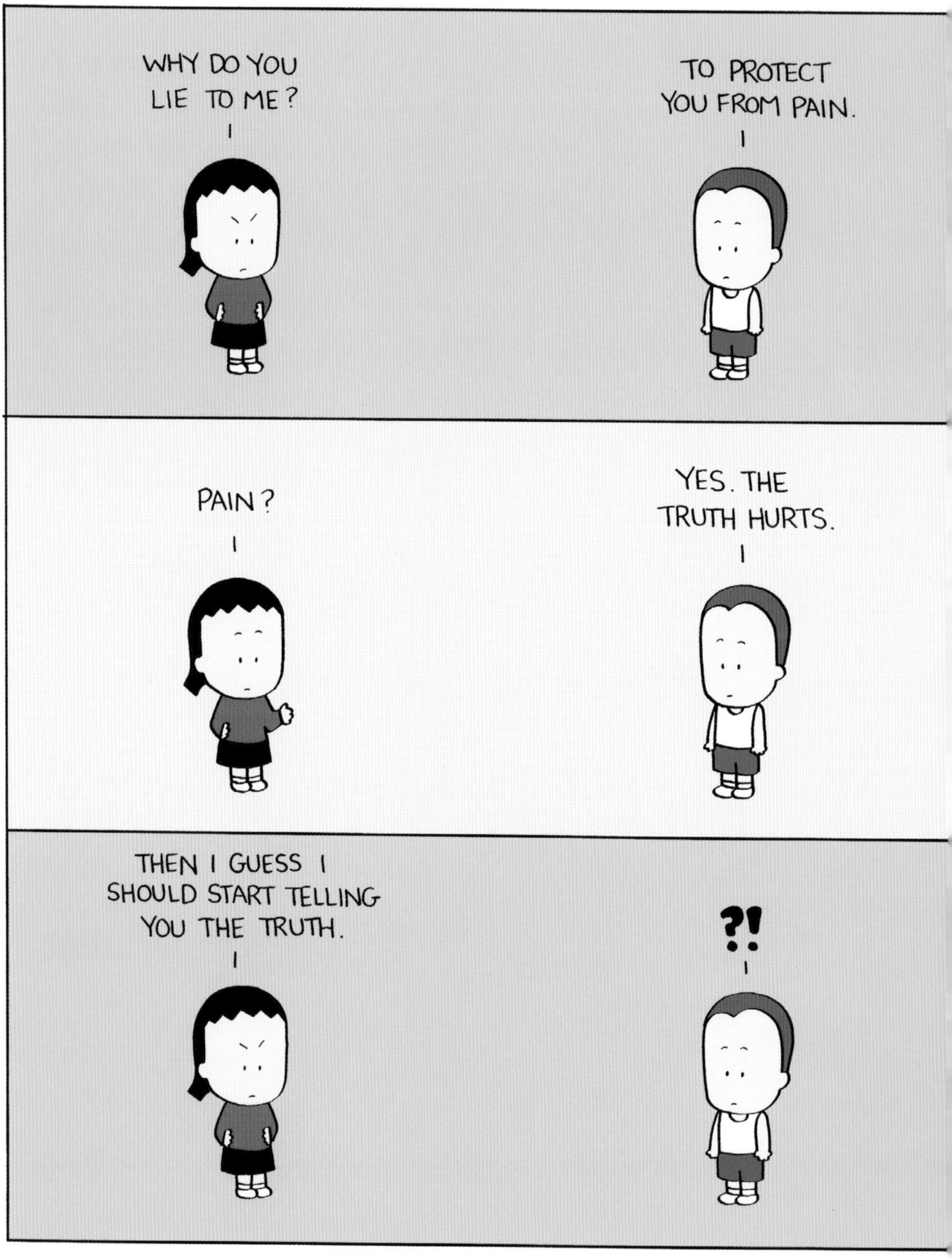
WHY DO YOU LIE TO ME?
TO PROTECT YOU FROM PAIN.
PAIN?
YES. THE TRUTH HURTS.
THEN I GUESS I SHOULD START TELLING YOU THE TRUTH.
?!

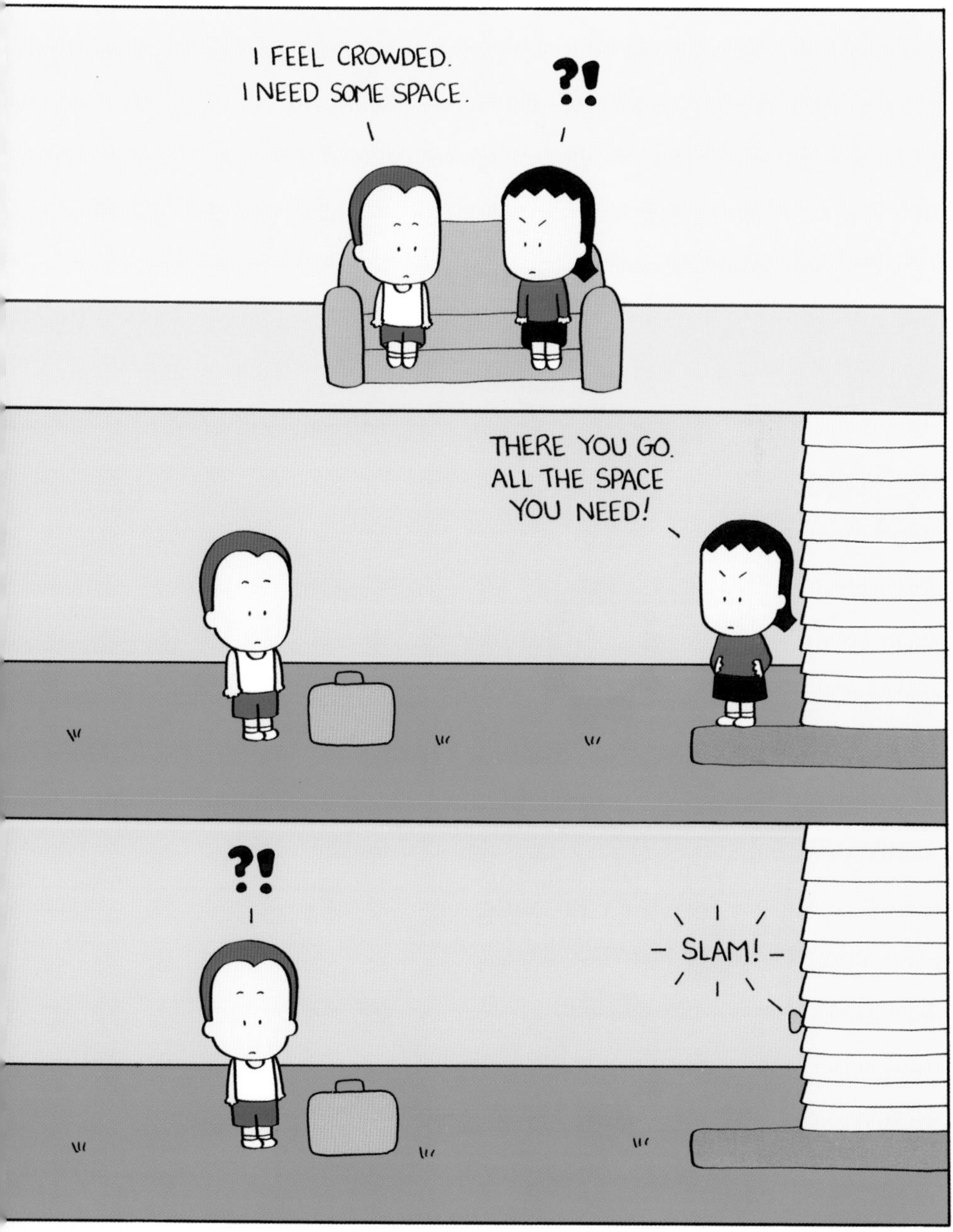
I FEEL CROWDED. I NEED SOME SPACE.
?!
THERE YOU GO. ALL THE SPACE YOU NEED!
?!
SLAM!

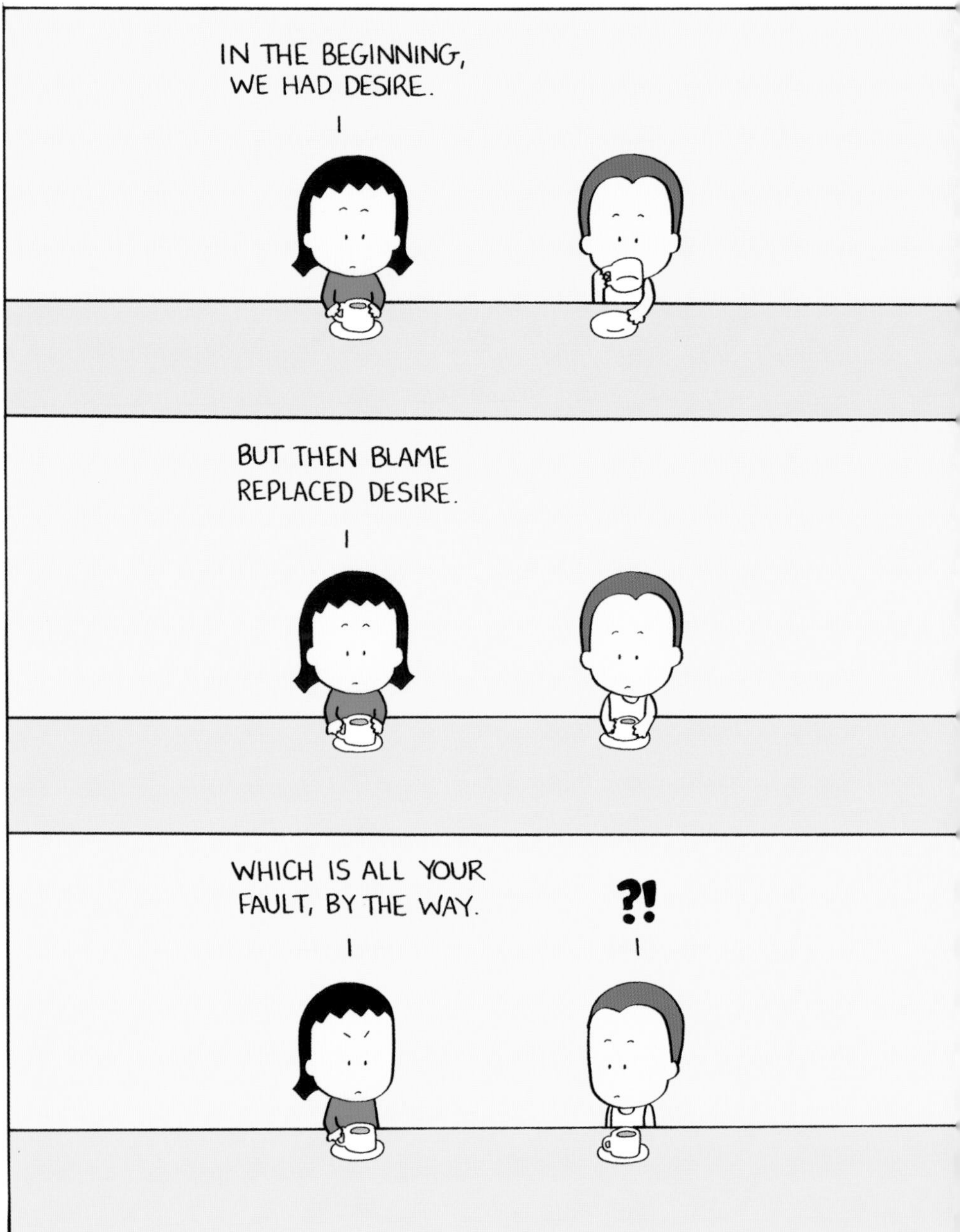
IN THE BEGINNING, WE HAD DESIRE.
BUT THEN BLAME REPLACED DESIRE.
WHICH IS ALL YOUR FAULT, BY THE WAY.
?!

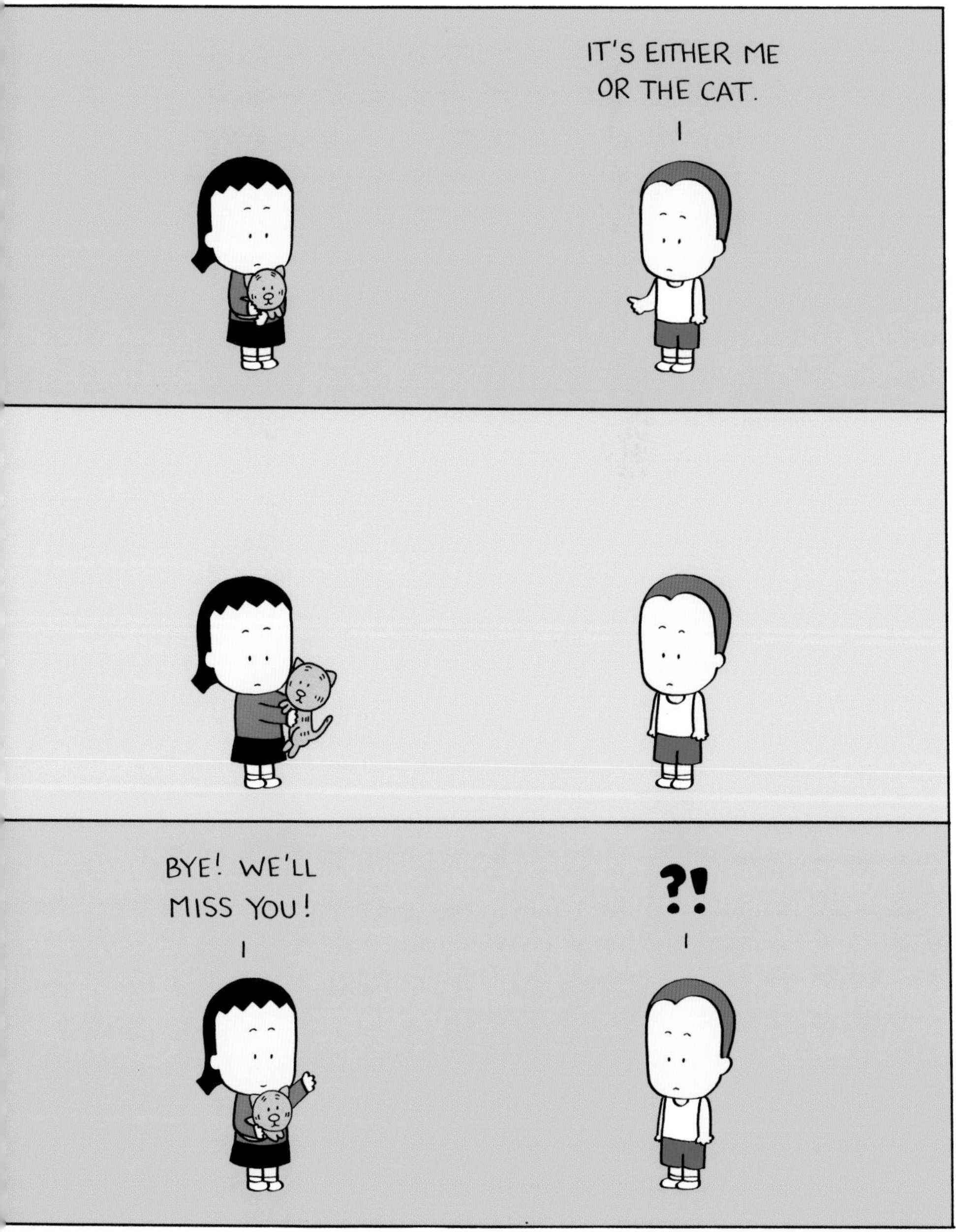
IT'S EITHER ME OR THE CAT.
BYE! WE'LL MISS YOU!
?!

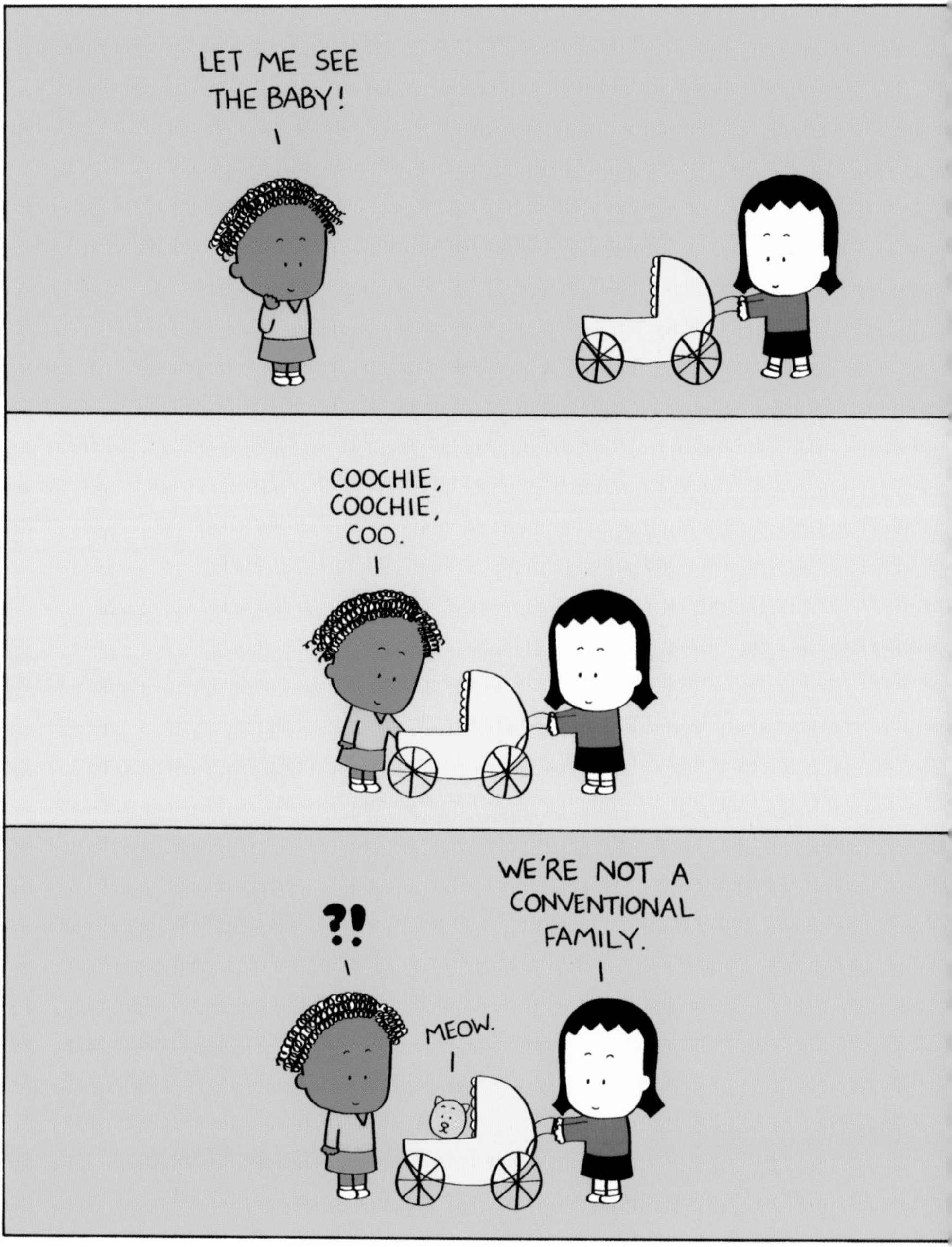
LET ME SEE THE BABY!
COOCHIE, COOCHIE, COO.
?!
MEOW.
WE'RE NOT A CONVENTIONAL FAMILY.

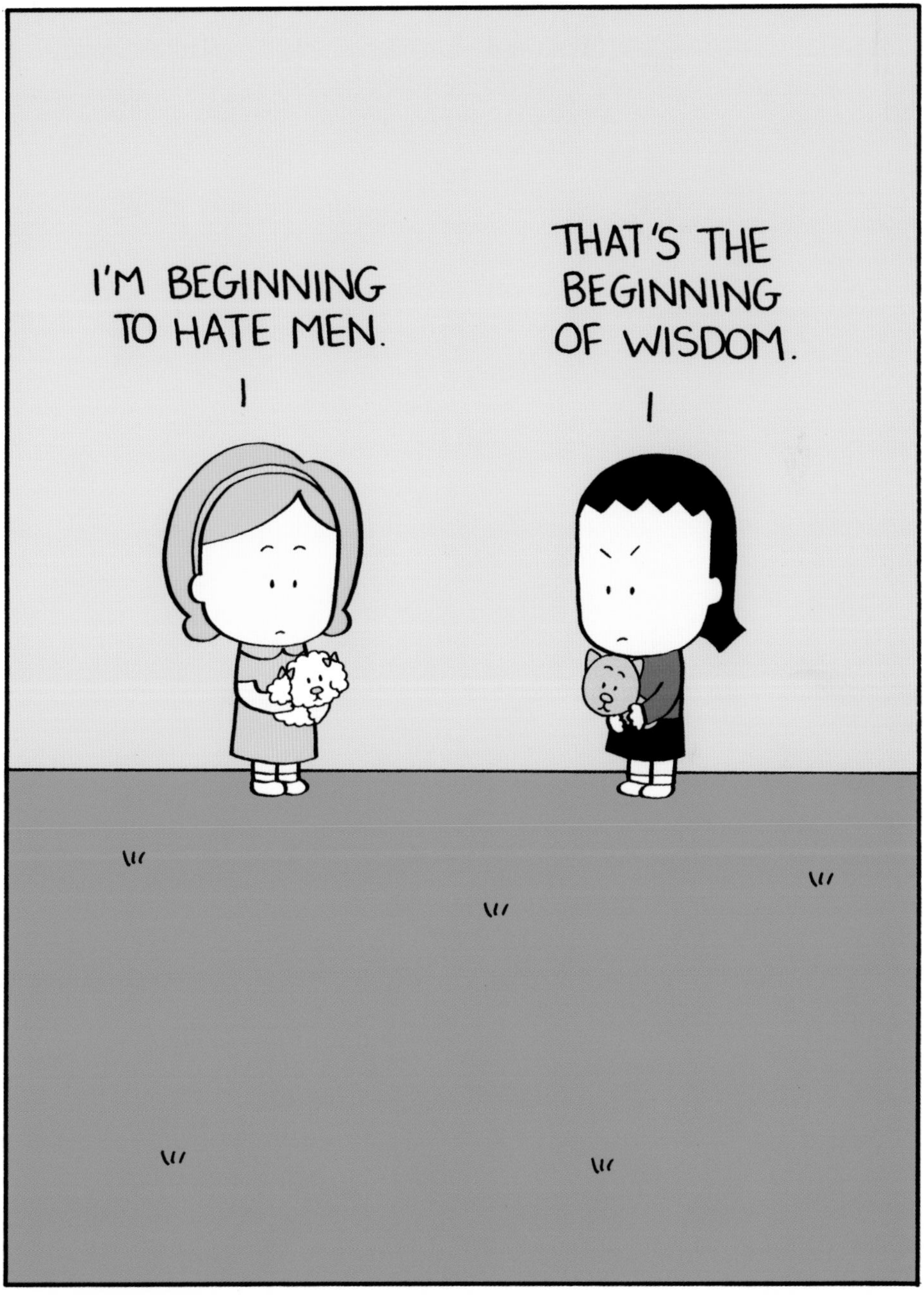
I'M BEGINNING TO HATE MEN.
THAT'S THE BEGINNING OF WISDOM.

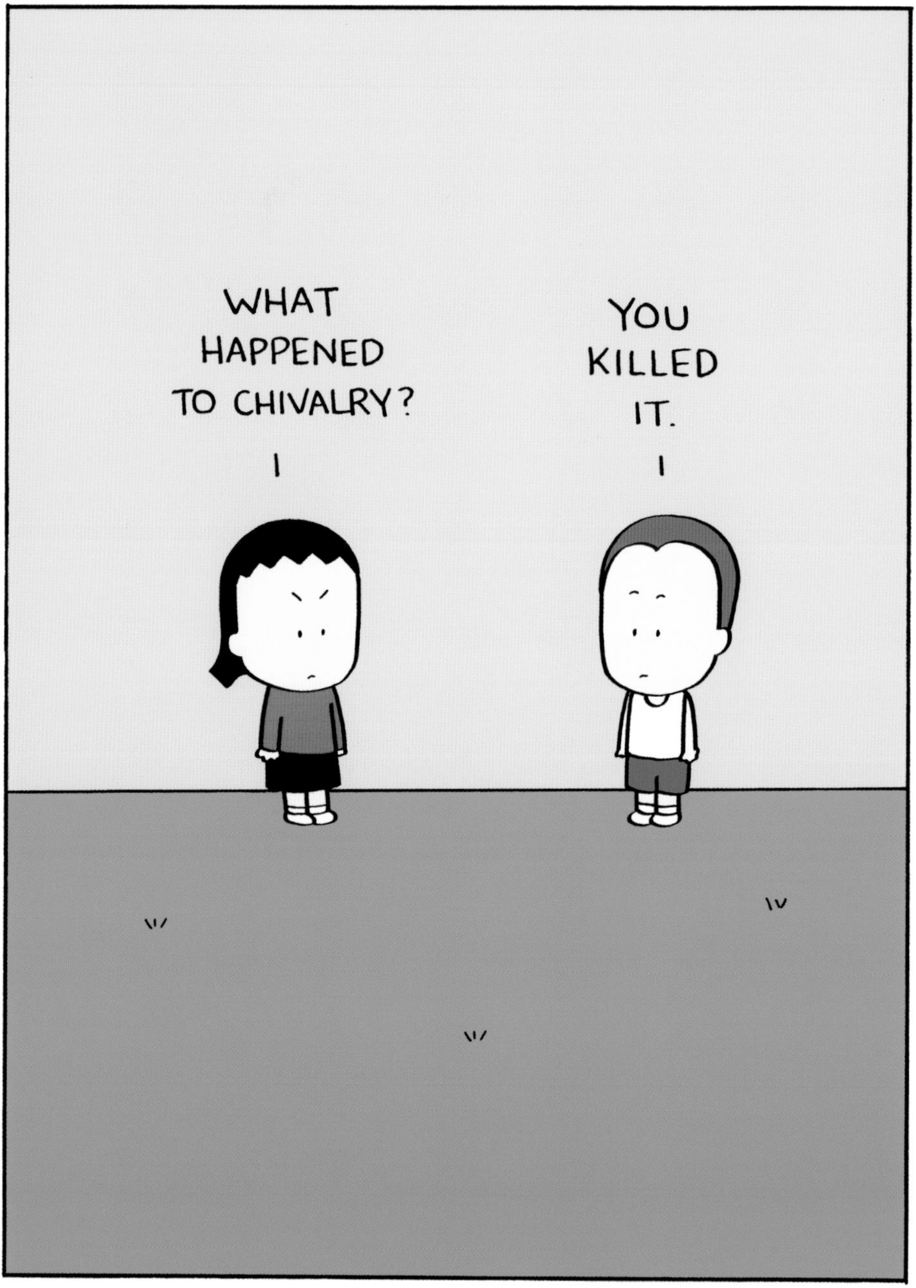
WHAT HAPPENED TO CHIVALRY?
YOU KILLED IT.

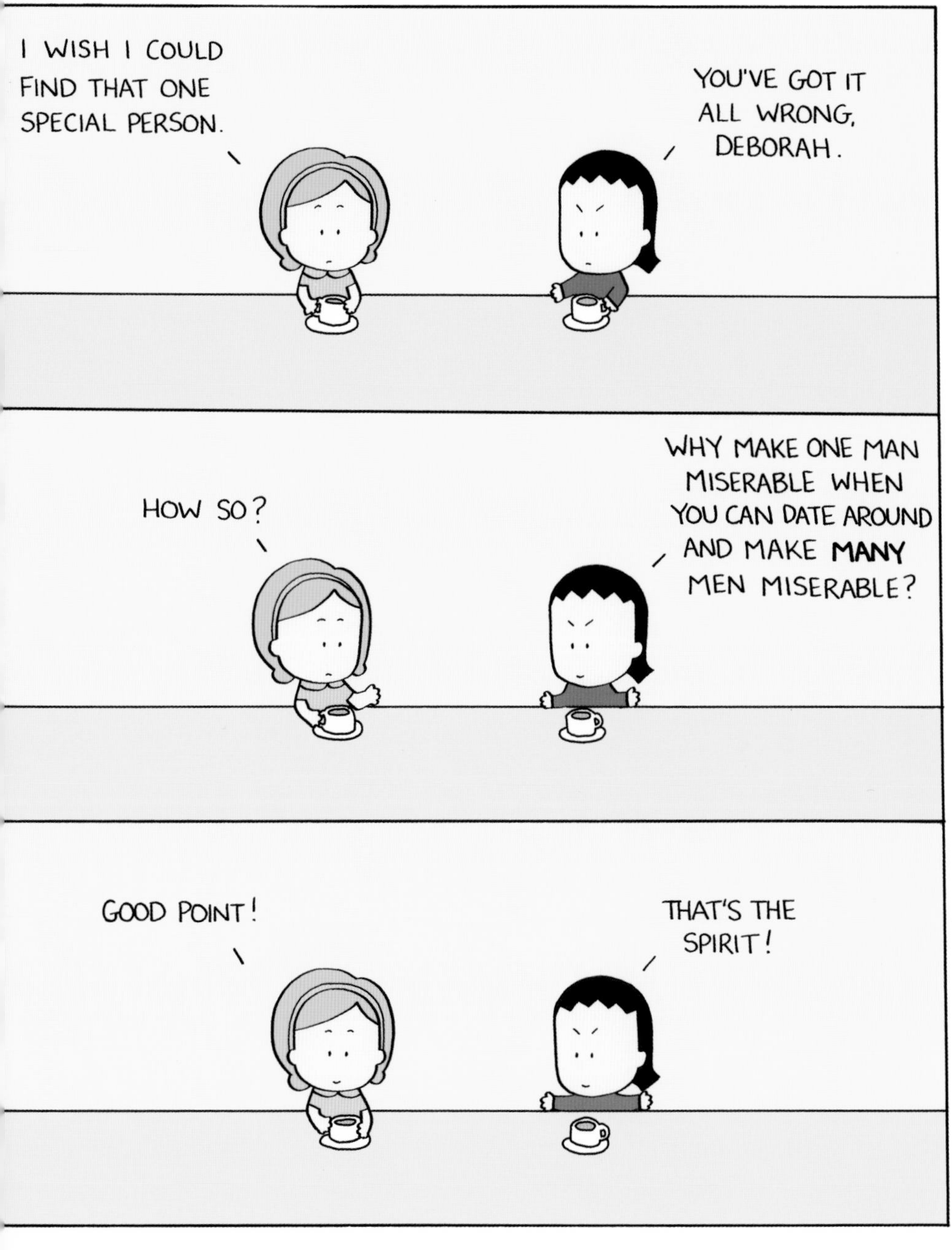
I WISH I COULD FIND THAT ONE SPECIAL PERSON.
YOU'VE GOT IT ALL WRONG, DEBORAH.
HOW SO?
WHY MAKE ONE MAN MISERABLE WHEN YOU CAN DATE AROUND AND MAKE **MANY** MEN MISERABLE?
GOOD POINT!
THAT'S THE SPIRIT!

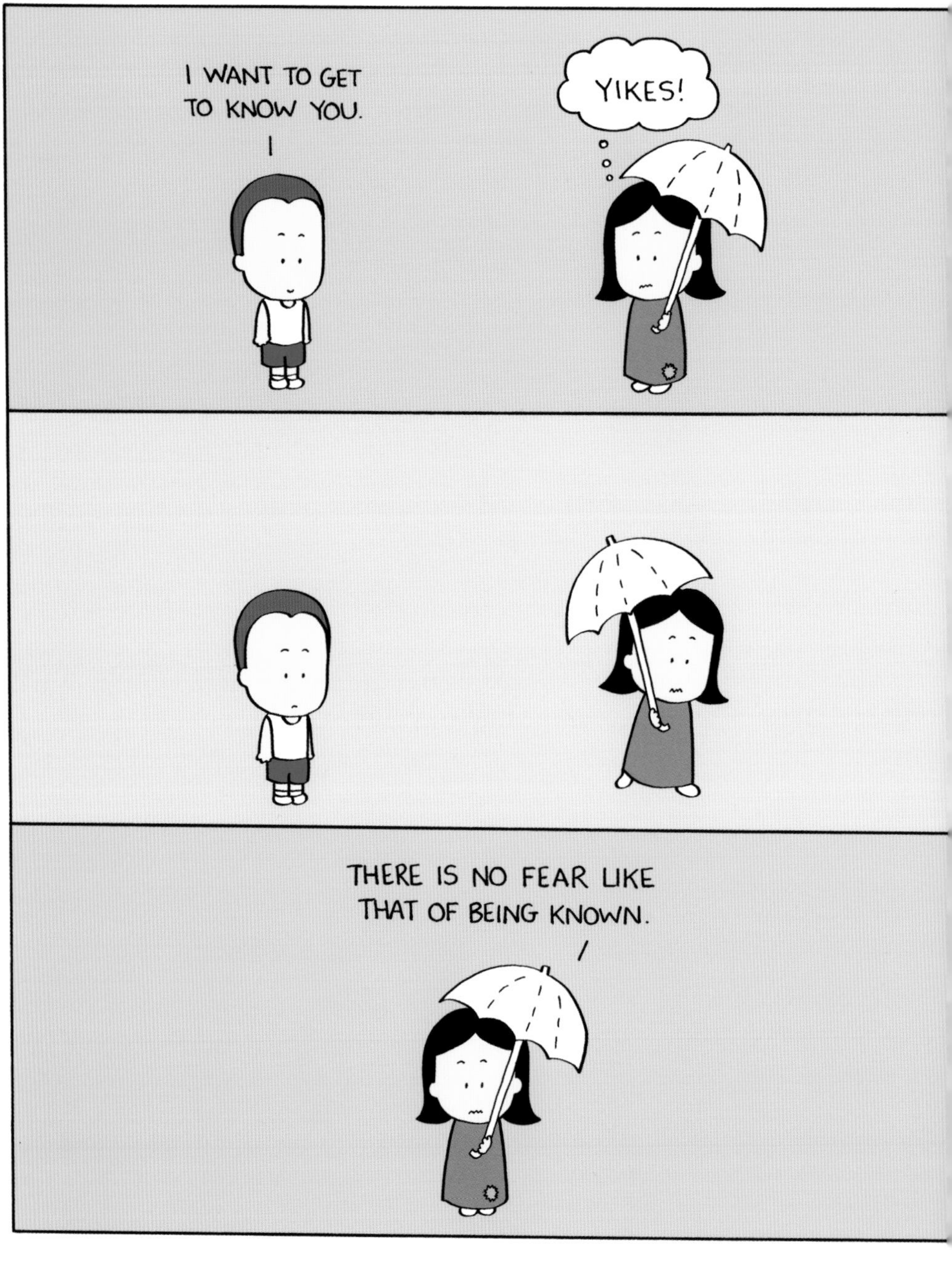
I WANT TO GET TO KNOW YOU.
YIKES!
THERE IS NO FEAR LIKE THAT OF BEING KNOWN.

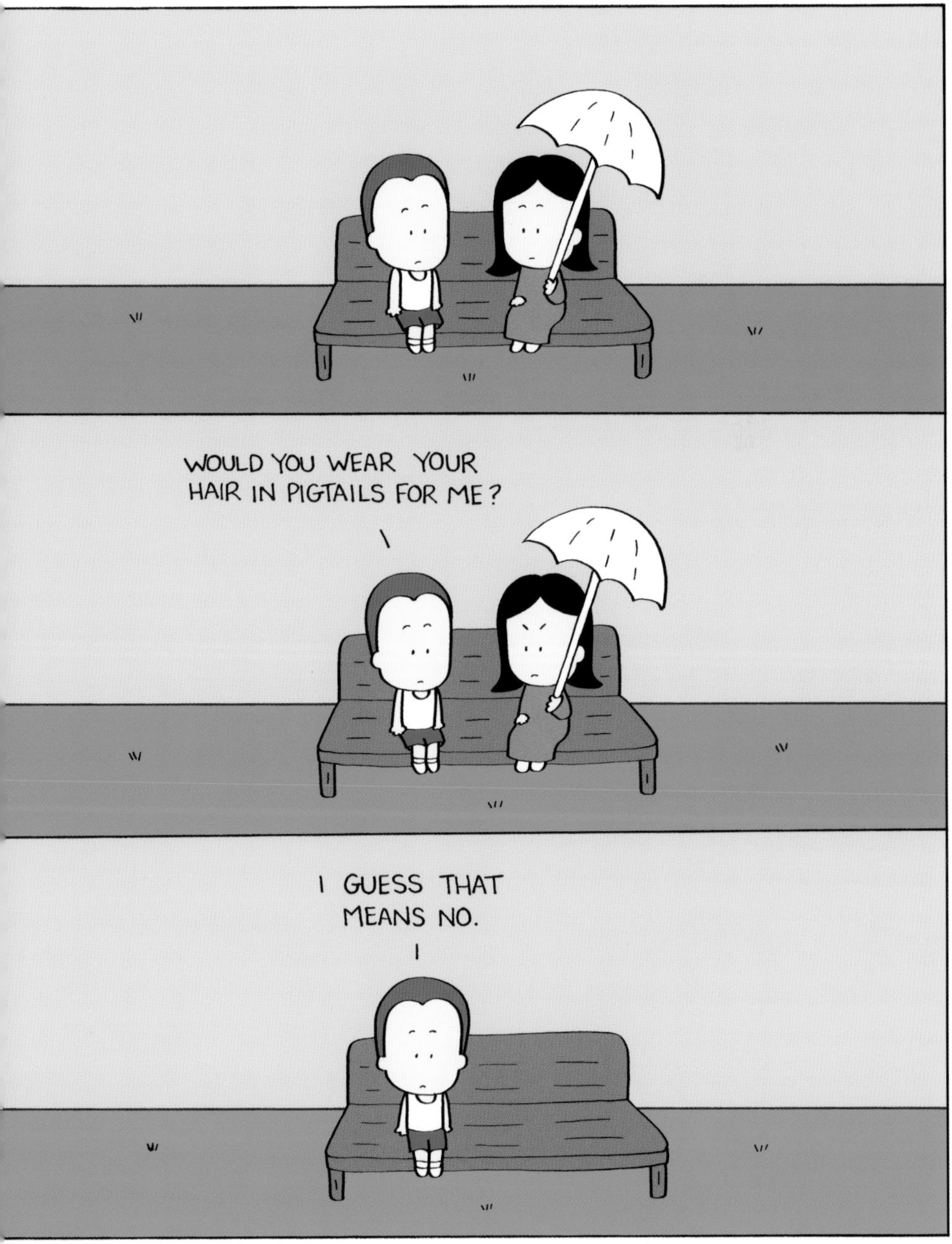
WOULD YOU WEAR YOUR HAIR IN PIGTAILS FOR ME?
I GUESS THAT MEANS NO.

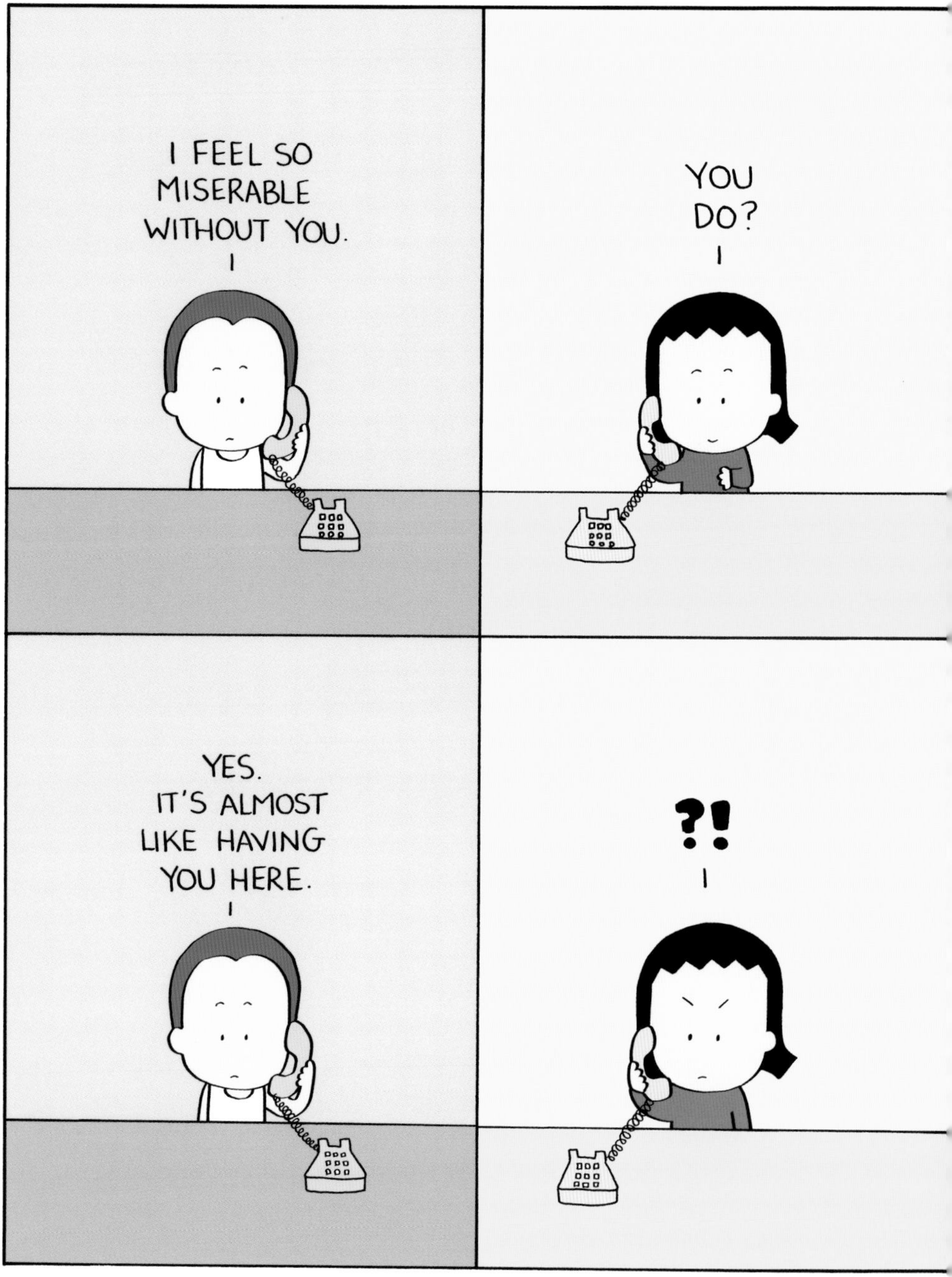
I FEEL SO MISERABLE WITHOUT YOU.
YOU DO?
YES. IT'S ALMOST LIKE HAVING YOU HERE.
?!

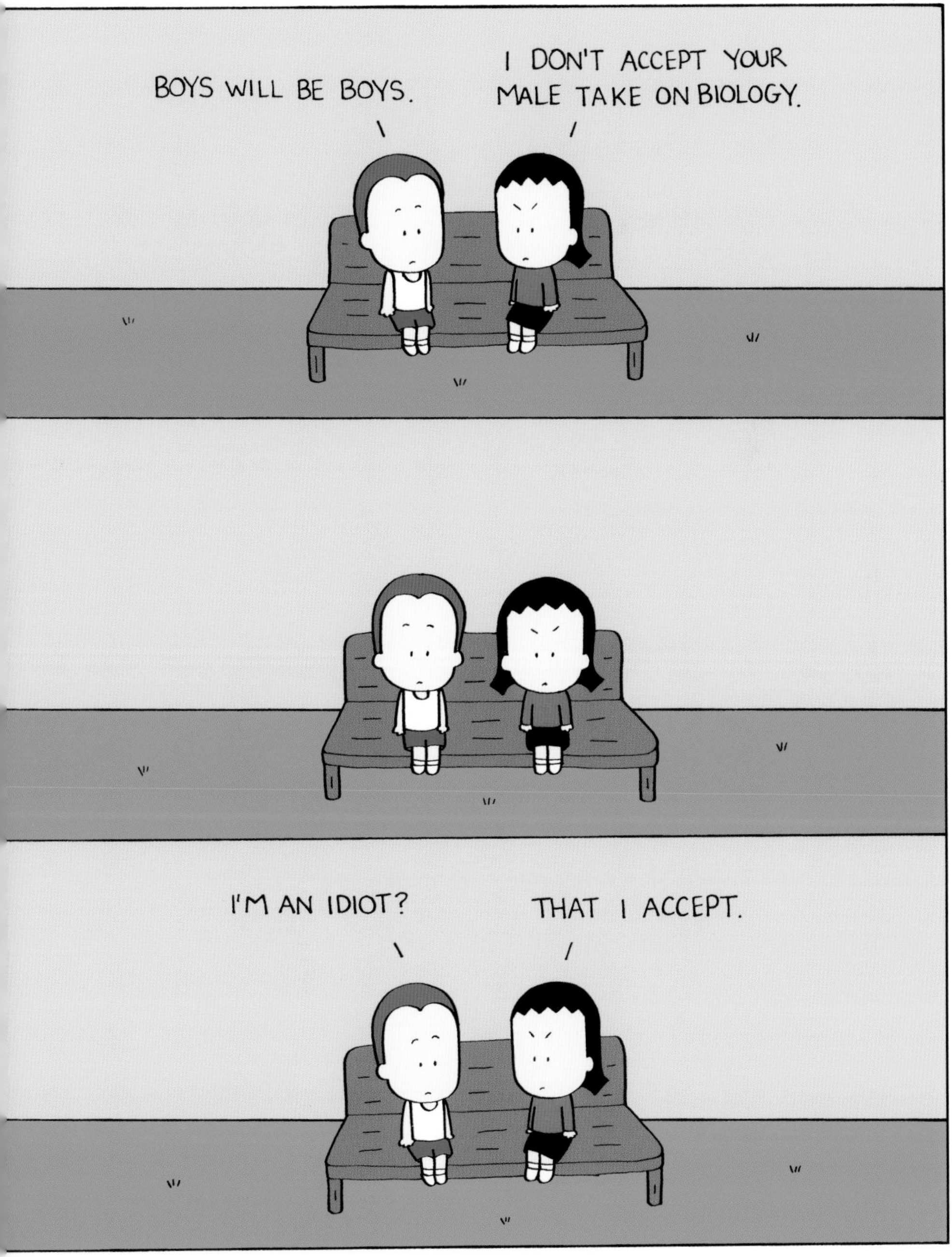
BOYS WILL BE BOYS.
I DON'T ACCEPT YOUR MALE TAKE ON BIOLOGY.
I'M AN IDIOT?
THAT I ACCEPT.

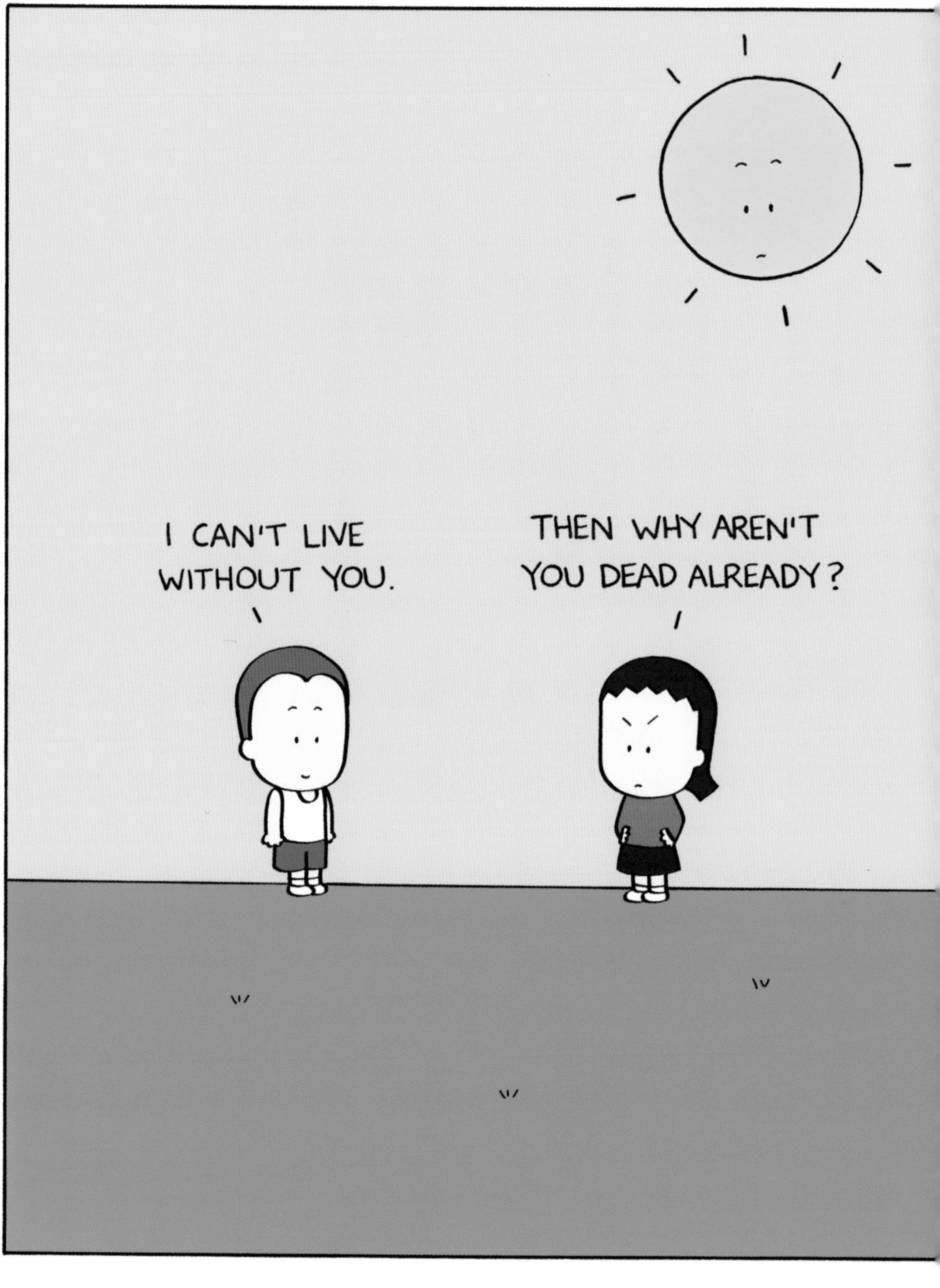
I CAN'T LIVE WITHOUT YOU.
THEN WHY AREN'T YOU DEAD ALREADY?

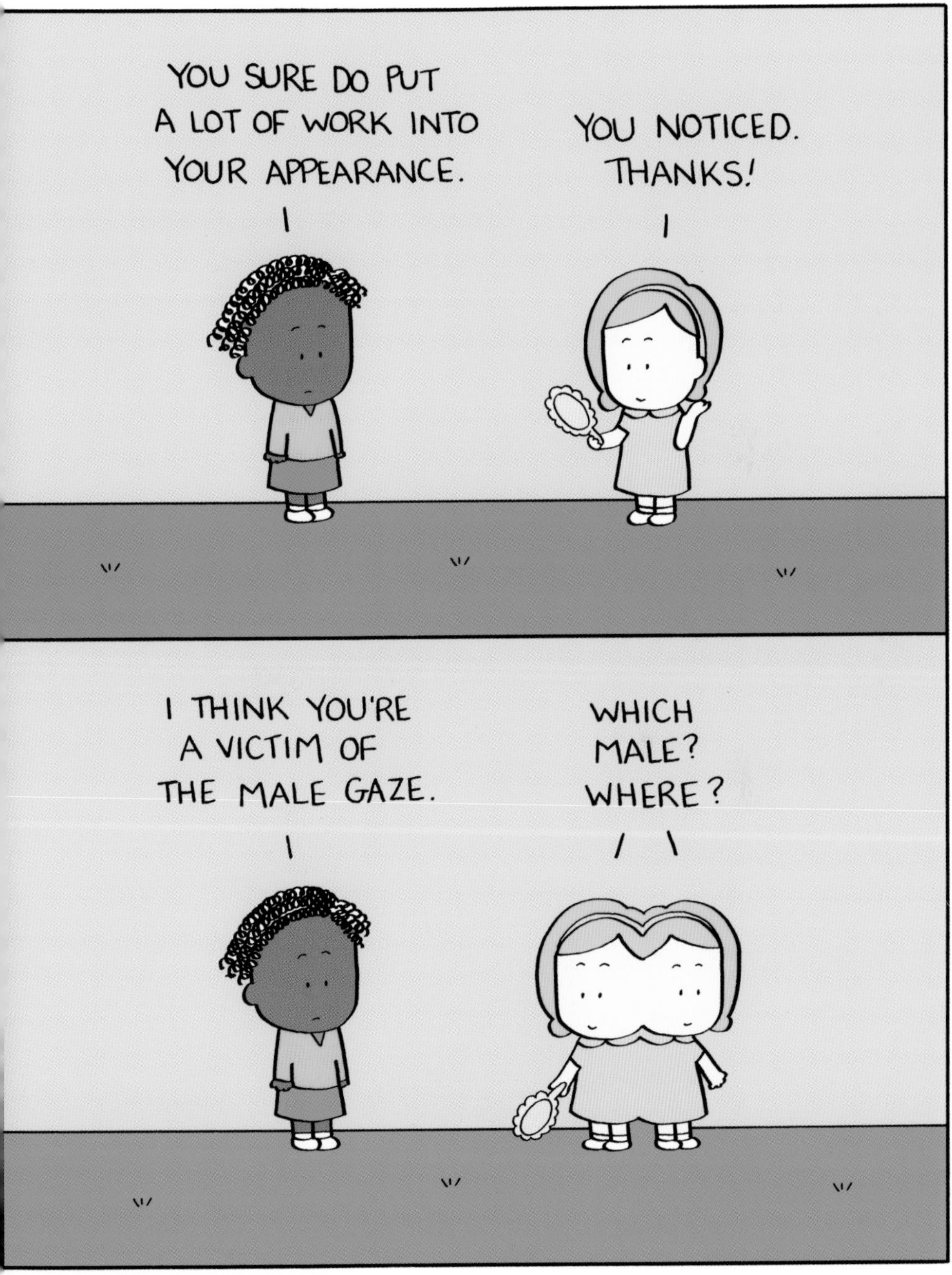
YOU SURE DO PUT A LOT OF WORK INTO YOUR APPEARANCE.
YOU NOTICED. THANKS!
I THINK YOU'RE A VICTIM OF THE MALE GAZE.
WHICH MALE? WHERE?

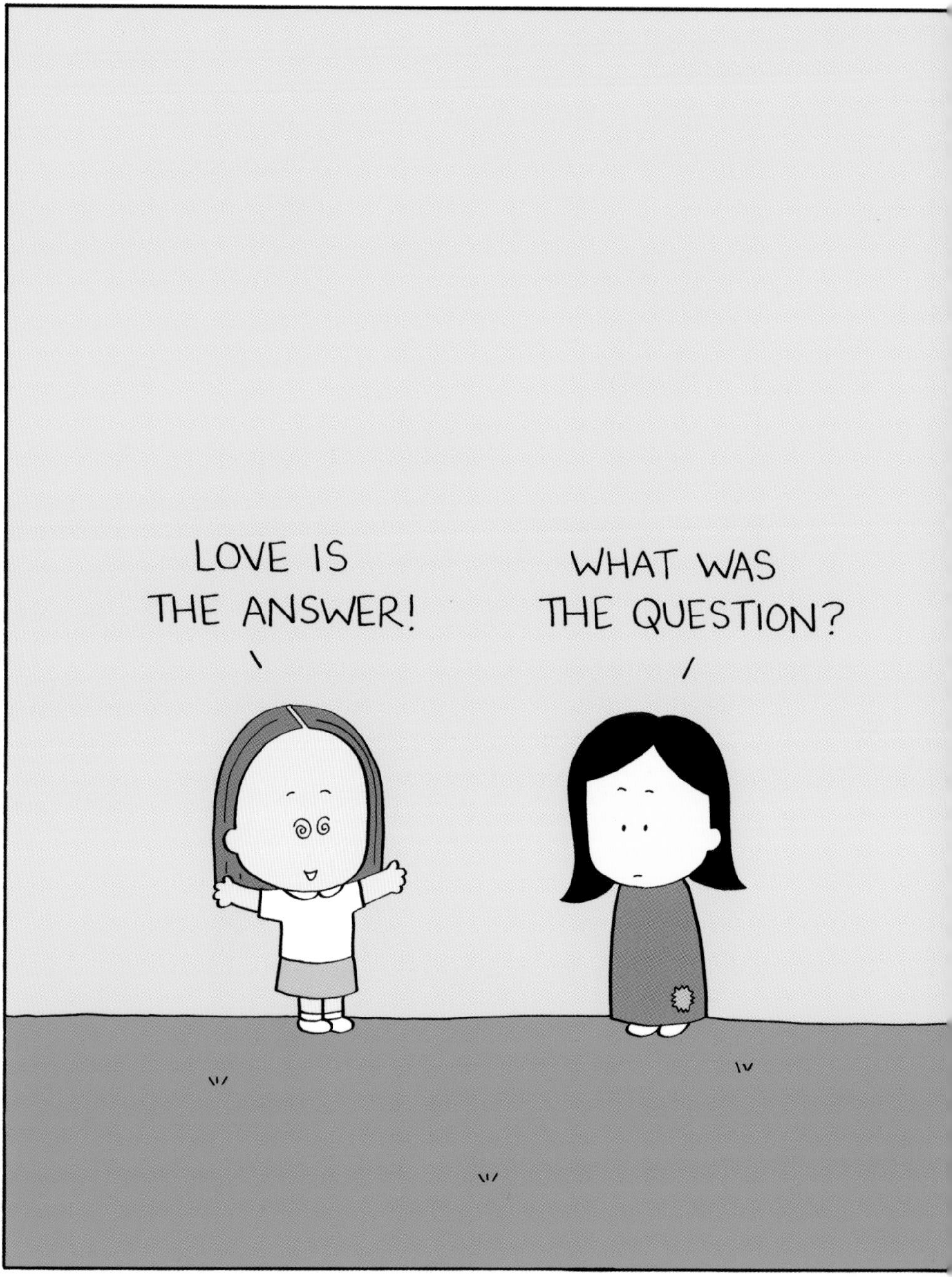
LOVE IS THE ANSWER!
WHAT WAS THE QUESTION?

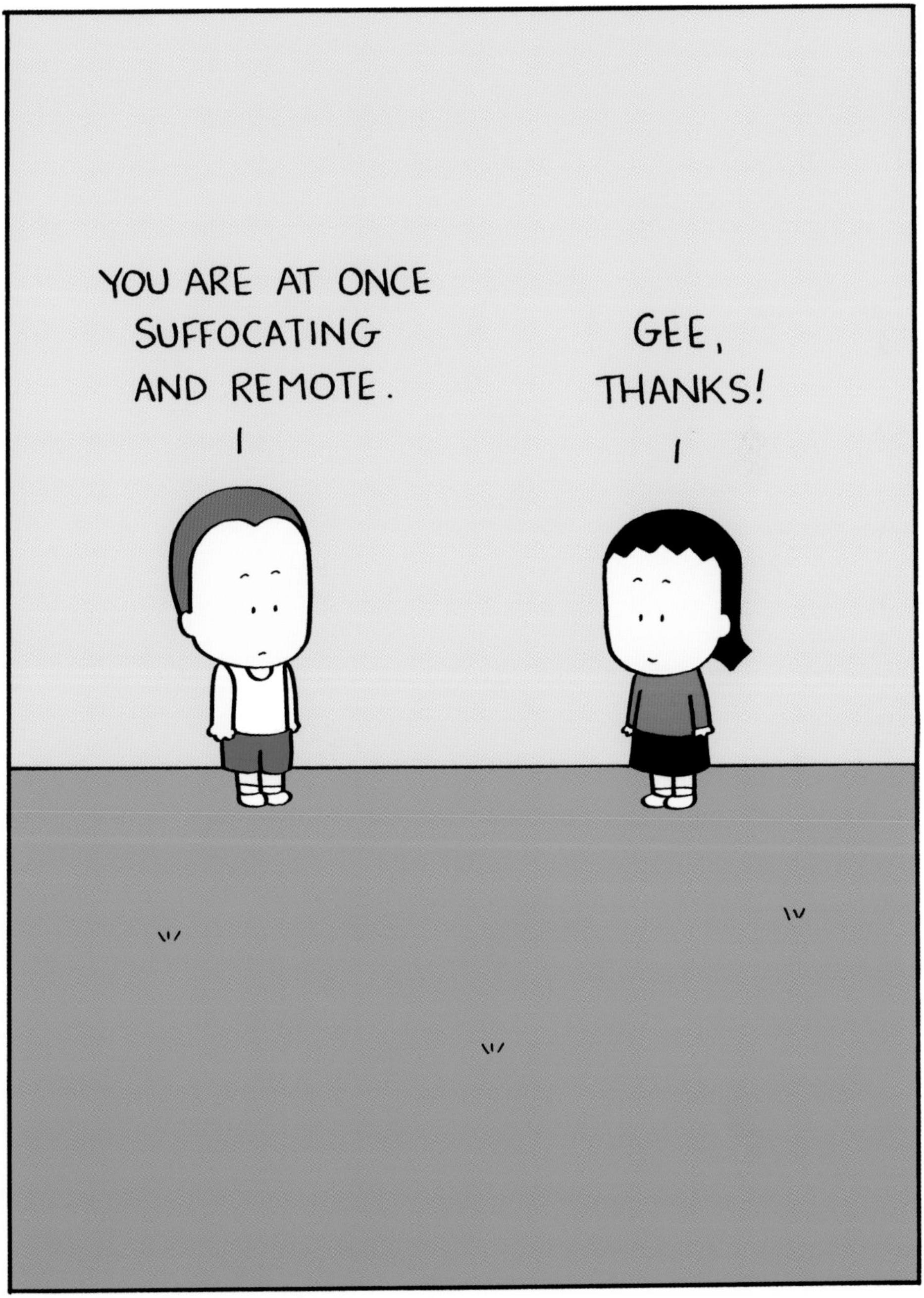
YOU ARE AT ONCE SUFFOCATING AND REMOTE.
GEE, THANKS!

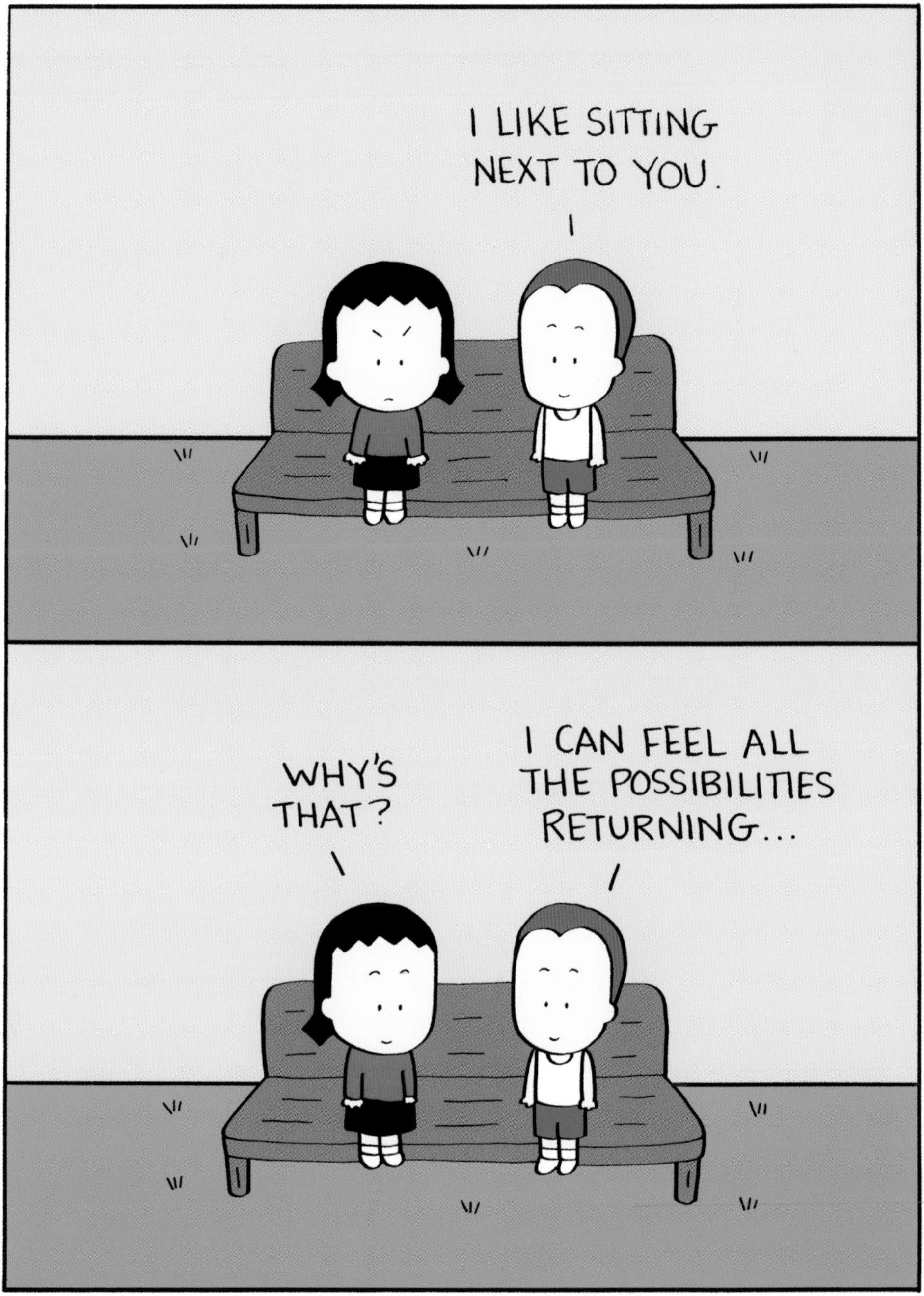
I LIKE SITTING NEXT TO YOU.
WHY'S THAT?
I CAN FEEL ALL THE POSSIBILITIES RETURNING...

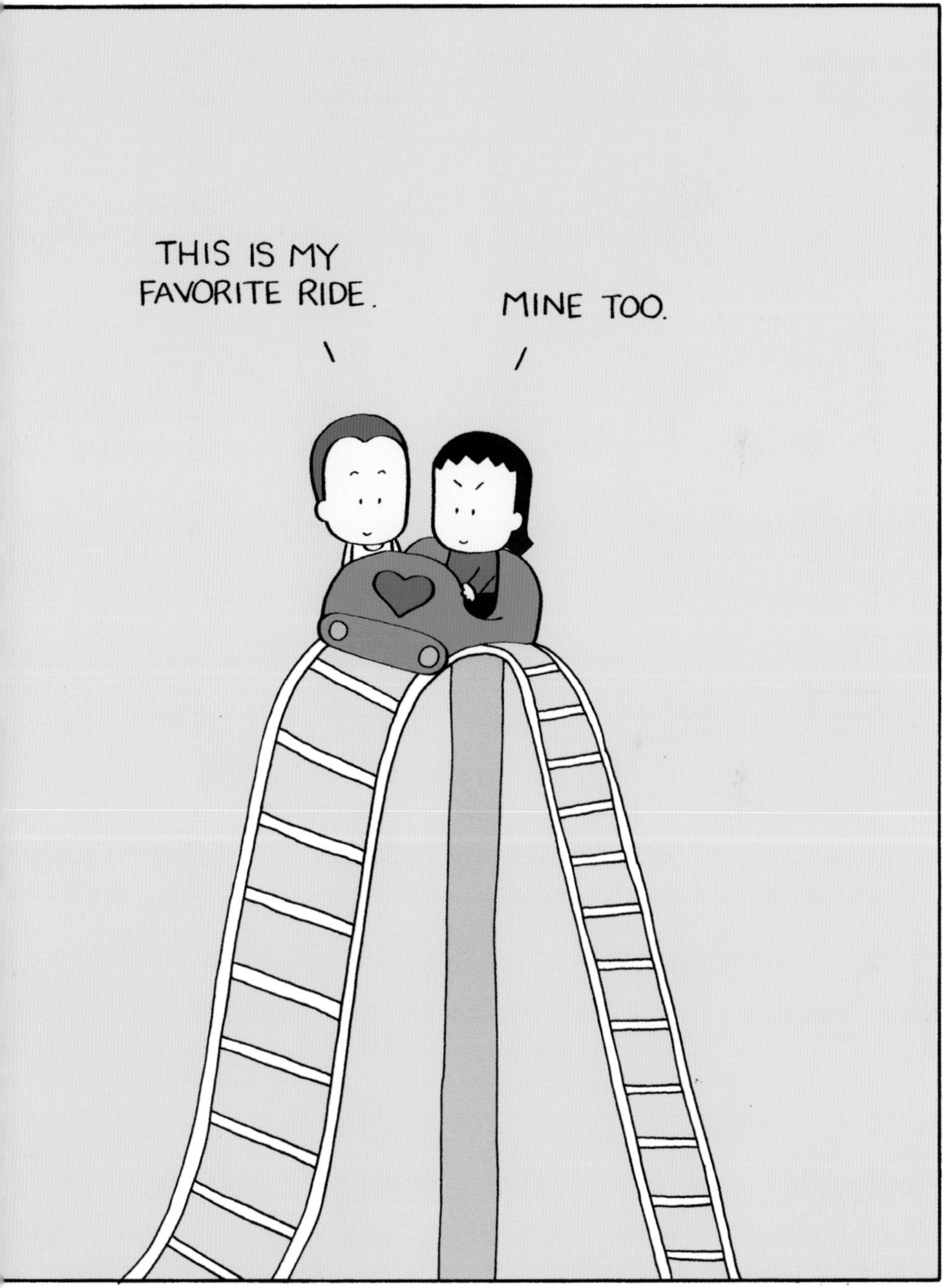
THIS IS MY FAVORITE RIDE.
MINE TOO.

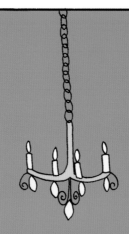

YOU LOOK
LIKE AN
ANGEL.
|

YOU LOOK
LIKE YOU
WANT
SOMETHING
FROM ME.
|

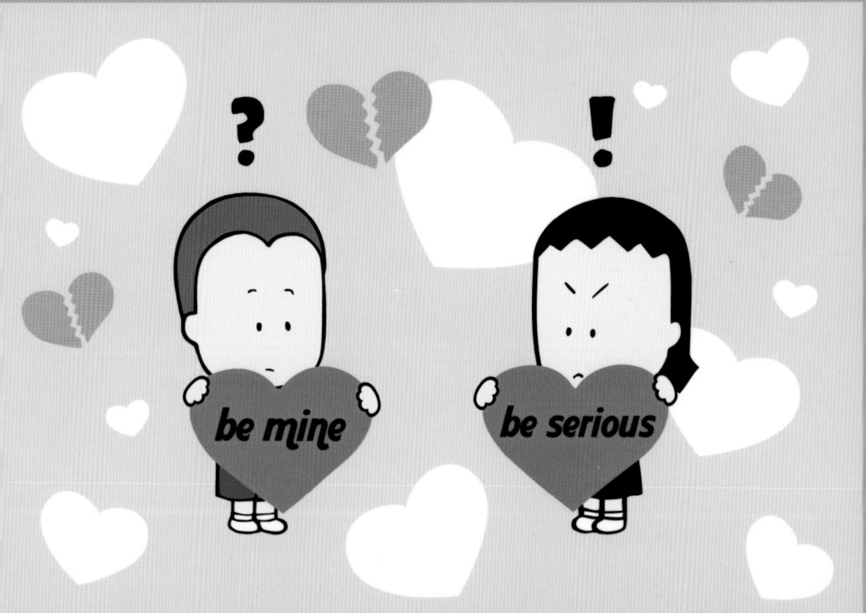
?
!
be mine
be serious

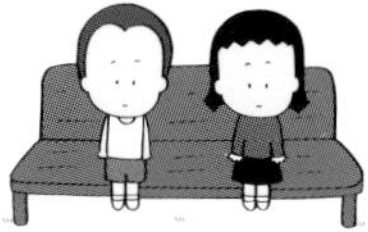

Post Office
will not deliver
without correct
postage

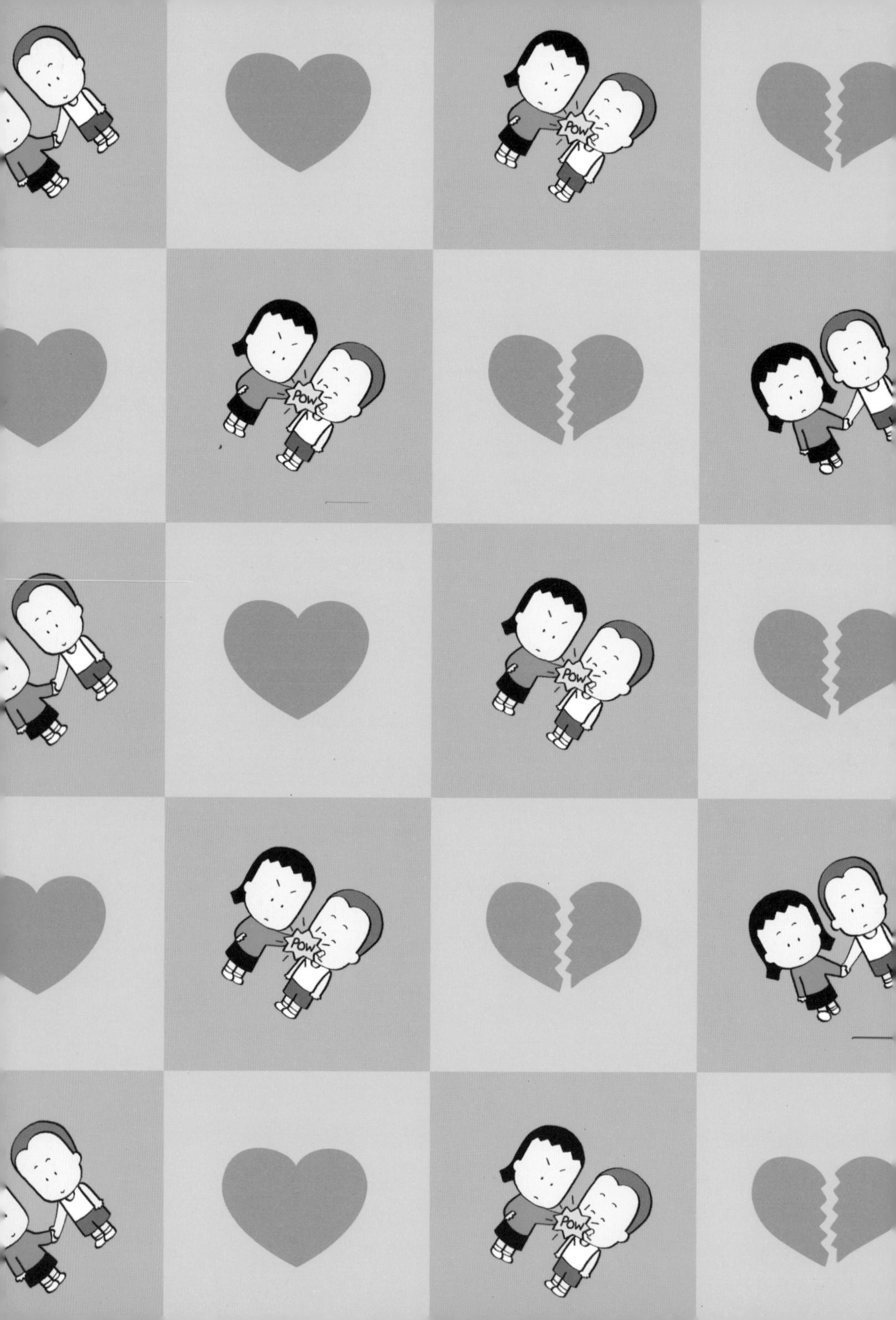
POW
POW
POW
POW
POW